Untangling the Golden Knot

Untangling the Golden Knot

CONFRONTING YOUR RETIREMENT WORRIES AND KNOWING WHEN ENOUGH IS ENOUGH

CHRIS POLLARD, CFP®, MBA, EA

mk1217 LLC

Chris.Pollard@GreatPath.com
GreatPath.com

ISBN: 979-8-9991397-0-2 (paperback)
ISBN: 979-8-9991397-1-9 (ebook)
ISBN: 979-8-9991397-2-6 (hardcover)

Printed in: The United States

Library of Congress Control Number: 9798999139702

Ordering Information:
Special discounts are available on quantity purchases by corporations, associations, and others. For details, contact Chris.Pollard@GreatPath.com

Publisher's Cataloging-in-Publication Data

Names: Pollard, Chris, 1981– , author.
Title: Untangling the golden knot : a guide to addressing the worries of wealth and knowing when enough is enough / Chris Pollard.
Description: Goshen, NY : mk1217 LLC, 2025 | Summary: This practical workbook helps individuals approaching or entering retirement transition from saving to spending with confidence. It addresses financial planning, emotional readiness, identity shifts, decision-making challenges, and lifestyle design. With real client scenarios and reflective exercises, it empowers readers to define "enough" and create a fulfilling retirement aligned with their values.
Identifiers: ISBN 979-8-9991397-2-6 (hardback) | ISBN 979-8-9991397-0-2 (pbk) | ISBN 979-8-9991397-1-9 (ebook) | LCCN 9798999139702
Subjects: LCSH: Retirement—Planning. | Retirement—Psychological aspects. | Financial security—Retirees. | Life planning—Retirement. | Values—Decision making. | Identity (Psychology)—Retirement. | Retirement income. | Aging—Social aspects. | Work-life balance—Older adults. | Personal finance—Retirement planning. | BISAC: BUSINESS & ECONOMICS / Personal Finance / Retirement Planning | BUSINESS & ECONOMICS / Finance / Wealth Management | BUSINESS & ECONOMICS / Personal Finance / Money Management
Classification: LCC HQ1063 .P65 2025 (print) | DDC 646.79--dc23

Table of Contents

Introduction

Dear Reader,

Does thinking about retirement keep you awake at night? *You have enough money.* At least, that's what your financial planner keeps telling you. You've met with them more than a few times. They laid out all the numbers and explained that your hard work and wise decision-making over the decades have paid off. You have plenty of money to stop working, invest, travel, buy nice things, donate to your favorite charities, spoil the grandkids, and even leave a sizable portion behind as part of your legacy.

So, what's the problem?

This book will focus on helping you stop worrying. You've already saved wisely and are either approaching retirement or planning to take the leap in 5 to 10 years. You need to know how to transition—financially and psychologically—from saving to spending. You must stop worrying and start enjoying yourself.

This book isn't for those who need to know how to build a strong portfolio or what to set aside in their 401(k) from their employer. Many books have already been written offering advice on how to ensure you have enough.

My name is Chris Pollard. I grew up on Long Island, New York. Seeking adventure and a challenge, I joined the U.S. Army Reserves when I was 17 before attending West Point from 2000 to 2004. The Academy had a clear view of New York City. I'll never forget watching the smoke billowing from the World Trade Center on 9/11.

I deployed to Iraq in 2006 after graduating from West Point and led an infantry platoon. I had initially planned to stay in the military and become a chaplain, supporting soldiers' and their families' emotional and spiritual needs, but I felt I needed a change in direction. Having majored in electrical engineering with a focus on computer architecture, I enjoy math, meticulous analysis, and planning. Toward the end of my service in the military, I became very interested in personal finance and investing. I had seen family and friends worrying about finances while making good and bad decisions. I felt inspired to combine all of my interests—taking care of others, applying math and analysis, and personal finance—and become a financial planner.

I originally started by working as a financial advisor for military officers and their families. After getting an MBA in Personal

Financial Planning and attaining the Certified Financial Planner designation, I served in wealth management roles for successful professionals, from doctors to inventors to college professors. I've taught financial planning at the undergraduate level. I also started and ran an accounting and tax practice as an enrolled agent, and, as of this writing, I am the principal owner at Great Path Financial Planning (GPFP).

At GPFP, we specialize in retirement income planning for people within five years of retirement. We serve business owners, entrepreneurs, and other self-employed individuals who have accumulated a large amount of the money they need to retire with little to no *mathematical* likelihood of running out. However, many of my clients express concerns that they could run out of money and "go back to the poor house."

I wrote this workbook because the path to enjoying retirement can be like a golden knot. It can be hard to pull apart and separate the things that hold you back—complex emotions, personal histories, and fears about the future. Above all, if you're like my clients, I wrote this book to help you *believe* you have enough to feel good about the next phase of life—retirement.

This workbook has nine parts and is based on conversations with soon-to-be and embarking retirees. Each part is divided into chapters, followed by a review section and questions and activities for self-reflection and discussion.

These questions are some of the same ones that I send my clients home with after our meetings. Some people will answer them with long, narrative replies, while others find short, bulleted responses are better. Others may find it easier to record their answers on their phones or even talk about them with a great listener. What matters is that you thoroughly consider the points and give yourself something to revisit when needed.

If you're doing this exercise with a spouse or a partner, I recommend completing it separately and waiting until you have both gone through the exercises before comparing your answers. You can be surprised by what you learn, even when the answers are from the person you eat and sleep with daily.

I use a handful of characters to illustrate the points in these chapters. They are amalgamations of the many clients I've seen throughout my practice. You'll meet Jim and Joyce, Sue, Martha, and Timothy as they navigate their own golden knots in their quest for happy retirements.

I hope this workbook will be a starting point for your journey to a more fulfilling and enjoyable retirement that reflects your true desires.

Let's untangle this golden knot by starting with your current life and where you want to go with your retirement. Let's find the right path *for you.*

Chris

PART 1

What Is Enough?

RETIREMENT IS A significant readjustment full of new opportunities and challenges. The time that was once occupied by your career is now suddenly free. It's a lot of time to fill, which can be overwhelming! Many people enter this stage and don't know whether they have enough.

When people hear "enough," their first thought usually goes to money, but it's more than that. Money is just one component of the retirement balancing act, which includes time spent with family and friends, exercise, travel, and more. As you navigate this new stage of life, you must find the right balance for everything. Finding the right time for everything important to you in retirement takes thought and perspective.

To complicate matters, there is no one-size-fits-all solution. What is beneficial for your neighbor might not be suitable for you. Your ideal balance today may differ in a few months. As you evolve and life changes, finding the right balance of activities requires continuous reevaluation and adjustment.

Couples have to strike this balance together. Successfully transitioning into retirement requires strong communication as they try to find the right equilibrium. They often have competing interests, needs, and timelines to manage. This was the case for two clients who came in to discuss their future retirement plans.

Jim and Joyce came into my office on Thursday morning to discuss their retirement. I offered them coffee before sitting down across the table to hear their story.

Jim had just sold his local chain of hardware stores. He opened his first hardware store at the age of 27, and by the time he sold his business, there were over a dozen stores. They felt a rush after seeing decades of labor come to fruition, and both were excited about this next stage of life. However, as they recounted their successes, they accompanied them with a list of hesitations and worries.

They had two adult children, Nick and Alice. Their oldest, Nick, was 24 and had ADHD. He needed additional support and guidance. They continued to provide extra backing and encouragement as he navigated adulthood and established his career. Their other child, Alice, was moving away for college to a neighboring state. Alice was thrilled to spread her wings, but this would be a significant transition. Jim and Joyce were excited to see their kids embark on adult lives, but the work wasn't over yet.

After staying home to raise the kids, Joyce reentered the workforce 10 years ago. She was now a mid-level administrator for their local library system, where she helped roll out and monitor new and existing programs.

She thrived in her role. "I just love libraries and being a part of something bigger. I enjoy meeting new people and learning every day," she said. While she was thrilled about Jim's recent success in selling his business, she wasn't ready to fully retire. She was getting back into the swing of things!

They wondered how to support their children while making their competing retirement timelines work.

Jim said, "We need balance to enjoy life while I am young and healthy enough to go on adventures and do things." He looked at Joyce and squeezed her hand. "But I also need to give her a chance to have the career she paused for our family."

I shared with them the strategies I will share with you in the following section for prioritizing and balancing existing commitments, unlocking new passions, and refining existing interests in retirement as you search for the right "enough" for you. Let's get to it!

CHAPTER 1

The Balancing Act: Time, Energy, and Life's Big Categories

WHAT "ENOUGH" OFTEN boils down to in retirement is time and energy.

Time is simply the duration you spend doing different things. There are only so many hours in a day, week, month, and year. Everything you choose or must do takes time.

You are now in your golden years. Over the past decades, you have tried, done, accomplished, and failed at countless things. Now it's time for a new journey, and how you spend your time matters more than ever. Like a musician finding the beat, discovering your tempo will require effort.

I define energy as the physical or mental effort you put into actions and activities and the return you get from those activities. For example, some people find that gardening makes them feel great! Other people find it draining. It leaves them feeling bored and exhausted after mere minutes. Similarly, one person may find fixing things around the house stimulating, while for others, changing a lightbulb will make them sit out for a full day.

In the same way that certain activities can contribute to or diminish our energy, some people can make us feel energized while others do not. You have probably encountered someone who left you feeling like a husk after a five-minute conversation. Meanwhile, other people can invigorate you after chatting about the weather. Most fall somewhere in between, depending on how much time you spend with them.

The quality of "enough" expands across all major life categories, which include:

- Health and well-being
- Human connection (family, friends, and community)
- Home
- Inner growth
- Fun, relaxation, and recharging
- Learning
- Finances
- Work and volunteering
- Experiences (e.g., significant trips or projects, "bucket list")

The goal is to allocate the right amount of time and energy to each facet of life. This involves reassessing and reflecting on how life evolves during retirement as your energy, time availability, and priorities change.

The appropriate amount for a life category will evolve over time. There will be seasons when spending extra time learning feels better, while other periods may demand more commitment to other life categories, such as community, family, or health. This requires that you be responsive to the needs of each season while still striving for an overall healthy balance.

The next thing to consider is which activities, situations, or people are avoidable and which ones are not. Paying bills is unavoidable. Landscaping your yard is probably avoidable. Seeing a doctor is unavoidable. Spending time with an exhausting neighbor is usually avoidable—if not, include a new, higher fence in your renovation budget for the year!

It's helpful to minimize time spent on energy-taxing activities and with energy-consuming people whenever possible. Preserving your energy and time for the things that matter most as much as you can is beneficial. There are several methods to achieve that. First, you can schedule your time so that those are the only thing you do on a given day or at peak times. Another option to consider is trying to offset energy-taxing activities by hiring them out.

Your time and energy are invaluable resources during these years. How should you allocate them?

CHAPTER 1 REVIEW

The two major resources of your retirement years are your time and energy.

- Time: This refers to the duration you spend with someone or engaging in an activity.
- Energy: The energy you gain from a particular activity, situation, or person compared to the effort it demands.

"Enough" is striking the right balance across life's categories with the right level of time and energy. Life categories include:

- Health and well-being
- Community
- Family
- Home
- Inner growth
- Leisure
- Learning
- Finances
- Work
- Major events

CHAPTER 1 DISCUSSION QUESTIONS

1. Go through the list of life categories and estimate how much time and energy you spend in each.

    a. Health and well-being: ______________________

    b. Community: ______________________

c. Family: ______________________________

d. Home: ______________________________

e. Inner growth: ______________________________

f. Leisure: ______________________________

g. Learning: ______________________________

h. Finances: ______________________________

i. Work: ______________________________

j. Major events: ______________________________

2. Are there any life categories where you need to adjust the time and energy that you allocate to them? Jot down some ideas for how you will do this.

____

____

____

____

____

____

____

____

____

3. Make a list of the activities that take up most of your time. How do you feel when you are doing an activity? Can you focus on it and bring your whole self? How do you feel when you are done?

4. Working from the list in Question 1, are there certain people and/or activities in your life who leave you feeling exhausted or electrified? How can you plan your schedule around energy sinks and energy givers so they can counterbalance one another?

CHAPTER 2

Examining the Present

IDENTIFYING WHAT IS working in your life can help you consider the right balance of activities while planning for or embarking on retirement.

For Jim, one thing he enjoyed was photography. Perhaps you volunteer at a local animal shelter, which brings you great joy (and dogs). Or you could take yoga classes at a local studio and feel good while making new friends. Other things that bring happiness include living in a much-loved neighborhood and feeling closely connected to where you live, belonging to a group (e.g., religious, trade, civic, or club), proximity to family, or overall wellness.

Identifying what isn't working in your life is equally beneficial. Perhaps you are dissatisfied with where you live. Many retirees have grandchildren, and some wish to be as close to them as possible. Others may not like the climate of where they live or want a smaller home with lower maintenance. You might have other aspects of your life that need more attention or changes, such as your health.

And sometimes, as with all big life transitions, people can't see what they will miss. One common challenge arises when social life is primarily (if not solely) tied to work. Time spent chatting and connecting around the water cooler is essential to their lives. It provides an avenue to develop friendships with people who share similar values and lifestyles. Outside of the office, they are isolated and struggle to connect with others.

A few things quickly became apparent as I worked through these questions with Jim and Joyce. They were tied to where they live now due to Joyce's career and thought they would move if and when they had grandchildren. For now, they planned on staying where they were. They intended to stagger a series of home improvements over the next three years, including new landscaping in their backyard, renovating their en-suite bathroom, and replacing their roof.

Joyce, in particular, was excited about enhancing their home. "I love our home and enjoy making it a place that brings us joy and peace. I want to share it with others and make it into a place that Nick and Alice can come home to," she said. Of their home improvement plans, she was eager to revamp the backyard so it could become a place for family get-togethers and neighborhood barbecues.

Jim had become increasingly interested in photography and was eager to start with travel photography. He wanted to travel as much as possible while he was healthy and could go places. "There is so much of the world I just have not seen," he said, adding, "but I don't want to do it all alone." Joyce shifted uncomfortably at this. She said she was excited to travel, too, but she did not want to jeopardize her remaining work years by traveling too much. This was an obvious sticking point between the two of them.

Outside of his business connections and a few close neighbors, he didn't have a wide network where he lived, nor did he know where to start. He had been extremely busy running his business and hadn't had time for clubs or many friendships over the past 30 years.

Joyce had a broader network of friends between work, church, and long-standing neighborhood ties. Still, there was more she wanted to accomplish in the next five years while she worked. She aimed to start volunteering in the community soup kitchen with one of her friends as a way to give back, and she was considering joining a book club.

Joyce and Jim agreed they wanted to spend more time with their kids. With Nick and Alice becoming adults, time was more precious than ever, and they knew that busyness would make it more challenging to find moments with them. They also aimed to prioritize their health by improving their diets and joining a local YMCA. Jim, in particular, emphasized the importance of taking care of their health. "Taking care of our health at our age is a full-time job. We need to prioritize it now so we can continue to enjoy our lives for years to come," he said as he straightened his back and smiled.

For certain categories, you may need outside help to understand your performance. For example, your health might need an outside evaluation so you can know how you're doing and what you need to prioritize to continue to thrive in the coming years.

Much like it is helpful to schedule an appointment with a doctor, it is also beneficial to schedule an appointment with a financial planner, particularly as you approach and/or jump into retirement. A good financial planner will help you understand and maximize your money.

Different financial planners will offer various levels of service. For example, I am the principal owner at Great Path Financial Planning, where we provide extensive assistance to our clients to help them holistically as they navigate retirement. I support my clients in living their best retirement lives, from managing their investments to assisting them in setting up their wills and trusts. Other financial advisors will have a narrower focus and provide a one-time snapshot of your finances and a targeted set of recommendations.

Wherever you are in this range of support, you need to understand and maximize your finances. It is valuable to understand a few things to ensure financial planners are trustworthy and will help you. First, how are they credentialed? There are many different credentialing licenses out there that can look like a wordy tossed salad. Second, how are they paid? Do they ask for a flat fee, or are they paid on commission for different products? Financial planners who are paid on commission receive compensation based on the financial packages they sell, which can skew the advice that they give you. Third, are they overpromising? If a financial planner promises wild returns on a short timeline, it is probably time to high-tail it elsewhere.

Do not let figuring this all out hold you back. You do not need all the answers immediately. There is no pressure, whether you do this alone or with someone else. These exploratory questions will provide direction and give you an idea where you should start your planning process. If you're unsure where you stand on one of the questions, skip it for now and come back when you're ready or have the information you need. I will be waiting!

CHAPTER 2 REVIEW

It is helpful to see how things are going in your life as you plan out your future using the life categories outlined in Chapter 1.

Some areas, such as physical and financial, usually benefit from outside help to assess one's condition. Schedule routine appointments with these professionals if you think they can be of service.

CHAPTER 2 DISCUSSION QUESTIONS

1. What does your home look like, and where is it located?

    ____

    ____

    ____

2. How is your health?

3. How is your inner and spiritual life?

4. What are your hobbies?

5. Who are the important people in your life? Are you connected to a community?

6. Are there things that you are particularly passionate about?

7. What else is working for you in your life right now? What is not?

CHAPTER 3

Aligning Actions with Values—Making Every Moment Count...Or, at Least, Most of Them

ANOTHER CLIENT OF mine, Sue, came in around the same time. She was well-dressed in a business suit ("dressed for court" as she liked to call it) and was prepared to discuss her finances. As we moved into broader topics, she quickly opened up about her current life and future plans.

She was about to retire from a successful career as a lawyer. Sue was a partner at a law firm and was excited about the prospect of retirement. She had worked diligently for decades to achieve her current success. She was eager to start enjoying new adventures and spending quality time with her friends and dogs.

Her transition was not without sadness. Her husband of 30 years, Frank, had passed away suddenly from a heart attack a few years ago. It was a difficult topic for her to discuss. They had been together for a long time, and she was still adjusting to life without him. However, his death encouraged her to seek a fulfilling retirement.

She lived in the home they had bought together 23 years ago. The house was steeped in memories, but she was overwhelmed by its size and struggled with the yard and sharp changes in seasons. "It takes me too long to vacuum the floors as it is. I can't keep up with managing the house every day. And if I have to shovel the snow next year..." she said and shivered. She was also a 40-minute drive from her doctor's office. "I really do not want to move," she said, "but I don't see how I can stay."

Two of the most important components of her life were her dogs, Keeton and Roscoe. She and her late husband had adopted them together not long before he died, and the two pups continued to help her navigate her grief. They filled her time outside of work. She loved to take them to the dog park and go on walks with them.

Sue maintained a daily meditation practice that helped her stay grounded during the last years of her career and feel spiritually fulfilled. She didn't have a formal workout routine, but she led an active lifestyle, took care of herself, and felt energetic.

Like Jim and Joyce, she was financially well-prepared for retirement. She wanted my help as a financial advisor, but also sought to maximize her retirement experience and sense of fulfillment. Setting up all the necessary accounts and transferring her money to the appropriate places was straightforward, but defining her plan for her life as a retiree proved more challenging as she struggled to adapt to life without her best friend and partner.

Beyond the time and energy you devote to activities, are you also recognizing how your core values and priorities are reflected in the time and energy you're spending? Ancient philosophers and existentialists talked about living authentically—aligning our actions and energy with core values and closely held beliefs.

Core or personal values are essential character traits that individuals find the most meaningful and often form a key part of a person's character. Common examples of personal values include community service, creativity, faith, leadership, security, and curiosity. If one of your values is community service, volunteering for your local community is an example of a possible activity to support that value. If your core value is faith, participating in religious services and being involved with other groups whose members share beliefs similar to yours are examples.

Priorities are those people and activities most important for you to engage in. Priorities may overlap with your core values, and they frequently do. Common priorities typically include family, status, home, health, learning, and friendship. If your home is a priority, doing renovations and upgrades as you can provides immense satisfaction. If learning is a high priority, attending courses at a local college or acquiring new skills can contribute to that priority.

Life gets busy, though, and losing track of what is most important is easy. One of the most common priorities that I hear from my clients is family and friends. However, finding the optimum time on everyone's schedules to spend time together can be challenging. Sometimes, despite saying that family is one of their priorities, my clients only see family once or twice a year. If that is the case, how can they shift that?

It can be similarly easy to lose sight of our core values in everyday life. For instance, a core value might be creativity, but it often gets lost in doctor's appointments, house maintenance, and all the other daily responsibilities. It can take some effort to integrate a core value into the rhythm of daily life, but one way a person could do that is by making time every week to visit an art gallery or take a class.

Sometimes, the things that fulfill our needs, core values, and priorities require a lot of energy. When that is the case, it's important to remember how much they give back in turn. Organizing a family reunion demands energy and time, yet it can also foster family connections, quality time spent together, and wonderful memories. Rebuilding a car takes time, energy, and study, but can provide learning, satisfaction, and community opportunities.

When it comes to deciding how to spend your retirement, the only person who can determine the right amount for a given activity is you. But sometimes, "you" can get stuck or head down the wrong road without a little help.

CHAPTER 3 REVIEW

- Core values are key traits that a person finds the most meaningful and often form a central part of a person's character.
- Priorities are those people and activities that are the most important for you to be with and to do.
- It's easy to lose track of a key priority or value amid the shuffle of life. Reorient your activities around your values and priorities to maximize your time and energy.

CHAPTER 3 DISCUSSION QUESTIONS

1. What are your core values? Examples could include creativity, family, community engagement, etc.

____

____

____

____

2. What are your priorities? Examples could include grandkids, a hobby, travel, etc.

____

____

____

____

3. Reflecting on your values and priorities, where are you spending too much time and energy? Where are you dedicating too little? Is it due to a temporary commitment, or do you need to adjust your daily life so that your values and priorities shine?

CHAPTER 4

Panning for Passion and Activity Gold

So, HOW DO we do it? We have a discussion with our clients about life—what life is like now and what it could be.

We discuss their lives, covering aspects from health to home, not just money or their fears. As we evaluate each facet of life, it is essential to express how clients define it themselves, rather than assuming what the word means to them. Health, for example, can mean many different things to different people. It can include how they eat, how often they exercise, how much they sleep each night, their other habits, and specific medical struggles and conditions like diabetes.

Health can also include mental health, which refers to a person's psychological and emotional well-being. Sometimes, individuals spend a long time managing difficult life events and long-standing issues without having the time or space to do so.

Another example is inner growth. For some people, inner growth can equate to intellectual practice, such as memorizing religious texts or deepening their ideas and values in other ways.

As I listen to clients, I pay attention to what I call "activity gold." Activity gold refers to a situation where a particular activity provides benefits in multiple categories. An example of this is when someone walks in the morning several days a week with a neighbor. Not only are they exercising, which helps their well-being and health, but they are also socializing by deepening their relationship with their neighbor. They also connect with their community through the neighborhood walk and their relationship.

We also aim to identify how to take the "activity gold" and reshape it into something else if something unexpected happens. If a client enjoys their walks but suddenly has a knee injury, they will miss out on physical exercise and social interaction. We then try to replace the activity that can no longer be performed with something similar—could they invite the neighbor to the gym and use the elliptical or exercise bike instead? Perhaps a swimming class or water aerobics would fill the gap. Identifying the meaningful aspects of the activity and finding alternatives enables the client to pivot to something that may meet the same needs.

CHAPTER 4 REVIEW

- Activity gold refers to when a specific activity provides benefits across multiple categories (e.g., walking with a group is good for your health and socializing).

- Consider the underlying passions and motivations of your activity gold so you can find alternatives if you're unable to continue doing it for any reason.

CHAPTER 4 DISCUSSION QUESTIONS

1. Reflect on your answers to Chapter 2. Where do activities, things, and/or people overlap to create activity gold?

2. What other activities do you enjoy, and what do you enjoy about them? Is there a way for the activity to be expanded to address different facets of life?

____

____

____

____

____

____

____

____

CHAPTER 5

Energy Versus Time—Finding Your Ideal Retirement Rhythm

MANY PEOPLE SAY that they are busier in retirement than when they worked. Work feels like a single activity, while retirement consists of frequently changing, shorter-term activities to jump between. Instead of sitting in an office for 40 hours or more a week, which feels like one thing, many retirees bounce between social outings, hobbies, trips, doctor's appointments, watching the grandkids, and more.

The pervasive hustling and bustling self-help culture tells people to wake up at 5 a.m. and do more (and more and more) every day. As one who started my career in the Army, we used to brag, "We do more before 9 a.m. than most people do in a day!" Instead of ceaselessly pushing yourself, take frequent opportunities to check in. Are you spending too much time beating yourself up, thinking you should be able to do 20 things before breakfast?

Guard your time and energy. Instead of pushing yourself to wake up even earlier, perhaps your goal should be to wake up by 9 a.m. and avoid drinking before noon. You may notice changes in your energy level and sleep schedule as you age. This is natural to a point (we'll discuss sleep more later).

It is also essential to remember that while something might not take much time, it could require a lot of energy. Seemingly small tasks, like calling an insurance company, can drain your energy for the whole day. Meanwhile, larger projects like planning a trip to Thailand can reinvigorate you. It is important to plan accordingly and find the right mix of tasks that work for you.

As you transition to retirement, your time and energy will fluctuate. Starting from scratch, you may have plenty of unused energy that needs direction and purpose. Take advantage of that initial burst of energy to explore various activities and make new connections. You may later find that you have less time and energy as your life demands shift. It's also perfectly normal for your needs and interests to evolve. Allowing yourself flexibility is key to enjoying this next period of your life.

As you do this, give yourself grace and permission to adjust the balance of time and energy you dedicate to different activities, and to settle into a retirement routine. This may involve adding things that resonate with you and letting go of things that are too taxing. The goal is to find what works best for you, and this process can take some time. Be patient as you explore new ideas and adjust as you proceed.

As you seek the right balance, keep your priorities and core values in mind when making decisions. These guiding principles will provide structure and keep you grounded, even as your circumstances shift. Your priorities will likely grow and change over time, and this, too, will change how you fill your time in retirement. Be open to the new adventure in front of you.

Ultimately, a fulfilling and successful retirement depends on what is most meaningful to you. There is no one-size-fits-all approach to life. If you can keep your time, energy, priorities, and values, you can create a retirement experience that is both meaningful and fulfilling. Embrace the new freedom and the possibilities to fill your days with what is valuable and meaningful.

CHAPTER 5 REVIEW

- People often find themselves busier in retirement than during their work lives.
- Create regular opportunities to check in with yourself to ensure you're progressing toward your larger goals (e.g., big trips) and align with your priorities and values.
- Health demands and energy levels change during retirement. Give yourself permission to meet your needs while aligning with your goals, values, and priorities.

CHAPTER 5 DISCUSSION QUESTIONS

1. How can you incorporate check-ins to ensure you aren't overdoing it while responding to your energy and availability? Do you have any "tells" that indicate when you are getting worn out or overdrawn?

2. What are some ways you can adjust your schedule to take advantage of your energy in the most effective way possible?

PART 2

Your Retirement Future

UNTIL RETIREMENT, MOST people have clear goals such as building and growing a business, buying a home, getting married, starting a family, investing, and purchasing a boat. But what about retirement? Your future can become unclear, making it challenging to consider your meaning and identity in this new arena.

Some people say retirement is just another phase of life—however, it carries significant weight.

It carries some finality: the end of a career, the last stage of life, while at the same time providing more opportunities with additional time and financial resources. This odd mix of finality and opportunity can be overwhelming.

Like the other phases, retirement will cause you to search for meaning again. If you attended college, you probably searched for meaning in your major. When you got your first job, you looked for meaning in your work. Finding meaning again without an externally imposed structure in retirement can be challenging. When you were younger, you needed to work to eat. Maybe your family expected (forced?) you to go to college, or you just did it because that was the next step. But retirement isn't a thing to do—it involves removing stuff you used to do, and instead, filling that time.

Think of your life as a bucket. Throughout your working years, you fill the bucket with work-related tasks. When you retire, you empty the bucket. This can initially feel liberating, but the sense of emptiness eventually takes over the freedom. That's when you need to fill the bucket with new, fulfilling things—not just anything, but things that have meaning to you.

This requires internal exploration in which you can fill the bucket with post-retirement activities that align with your values. Random hobbies and travel destinations won't fill the bucket. However, hobbies that resonate with you and visiting places you have always wanted to see will provide the purpose you might be seeking.

Sometimes, it can be hard to devise a plan to vet new activities in a manageable way or see where you need further brainstorming. Begin thinking about things you would like to try in retirement at least one to three years before you stop working. It is rare for anybody to jump into retirement without a plan and make it stick on the first attempt. Therefore, if you have time, try a few activities before retiring to see what works.

I spoke with Jim and Joyce about their retirement future.

"What is something you have always wanted to do?" I began by asking them.

Joyce immediately responded, "I am already doing what I always wanted to do! It feels like I have reached a great point in my career, and I love that it gives back to the community. Every day feels like a stretch. I am so happy to have more of Jim's time now and watch Alice and Nick thrive."

Jim took a bit longer to respond. "I am also finding it hard to step down from my position to nothing," he admitted. "I was always focused on work, so now I am unsure what is supposed to come next. I feel like I have no milestones or things to reach now. Sure, I have hobbies, but they are not the same."

This feeling is familiar to those used to work filling every corner of their lives. This is especially true for individuals who held C-suite and entrepreneurship roles, as they are accustomed to managing significant workloads and inspiring people through their passion and leadership. I had a client who was the head of a cardiovascular clinic who had difficulty finding purpose after retirement. Much like Jim, he also had a tough time adjusting. "I used to be a doctor, and now I am nobody," he said, struggling with the new time he had in his life.

Another client and I had a conversation about his recent retirement. He said, "It is the hardest thing I have ever done." This client had an incredibly disciplined personality, served in the military, deployed in combat, and built a successful business that resulted in a net worth in the millions. Yet he thought finding purpose and meaning in retirement was tough!

Figuring out your right path through retirement is something only you can do. For some people, it is simple. They know deep down what they want to do, and when retirement comes, they are ready. One of my clients had always wanted to get into beekeeping. That was the only thing she was interested in, so when she retired, she dove straight in. A few hives and classes later, she was a happy camper. Easy enough!

Or there are a lot of things that you want to do. Some benefit from trying out many activities and seeing which ones feel right. This can take longer, particularly since every new skill has a learning curve, but it can yield surprising and exciting results. This was the case for another one of my clients whose interests spread from

Japanese floral arrangements to cycling. For this person, providing space over a few years so they could explore each of these interests helped them discover parts of themselves that work had previously left unfilled.

It can be challenging for others to identify and nail down what they want. And what you need and want changes over time, so it often feels like a moving target.

This section will explore how you can plan your retirement future for success. Many people struggle with retirement, but a clear vision and knowledge will help ease the way!

CHAPTER 6

Minding the Gaps When Stepping Into Retirement

CAREERS SERVE US in many ways beyond just financial benefits. They can challenge, inspire, and drive us. In short, they can keep us growing. If you are like Jim and are struggling with the transition to retirement, it helps to identify what you specifically miss or what gaps exist in retirement. Do you always miss having a full plate? Your importance in your field? Mentoring others or, perhaps, holding a leadership position?

This is also a time when many people struggle to adapt to an empty nest as their children become fully fledged adults. Maybe you are experiencing that ache and missing the act of caring for others.

This can make the retirement transition difficult as we struggle to find new ways to fill those gaps. What could scratch that itch in retirement short of returning to work full-time? Could the person open a consultancy practice or volunteer, or is it something else? If the retiree mostly misses being in a position of leadership, then would being a director at an animal shelter fit the bill, or would serving on a prominent board be a better fit? What does it mean to "be somebody"?

I asked Jim these questions, and he gave me a few examples of what he missed in his career. First, he shared how he found a talented person whose career he had helped grow. She had started as a cashier in one of his stores over a decade ago while also studying for her business degree. He was impressed by her work ethic and provided opportunities for her to excel.

Soon, she managed a store and gave him valuable ideas for expanding his hardware business in the internet age. If he had not spotted her drive and business acumen early on, he would not have been able to sell his stores and retire comfortably. He loved finding eager and hard-working people to bring up through his businesses to reach success.

He also described the overall tempo of being a business owner. He would frequently work long hours and weekends, particularly during his busy times of the year. Jim was always on the go, trying new programs, systematizing and making existing processes more efficient, and securing new funding when it was time to expand. He kept an idea pad on his nightstand where he would write out different plans as they came to him before he fell asleep.

"Now I never have ideas to put into my idea book. There is no point in it anyway," he said glumly.

In short, we whittled down the list of things Jim missed to mentoring up-and-coming talent and the day-to-day busyness of entrepreneurial life.

After we pinpointed what he was missing, we brainstormed a list of activities for him to try out. We wanted to determine whether other activities would provide fulfillment while allowing time with family, travel, and practicing photography. A few ideas we thought up included joining a program to mentor young entrepreneurs, applying for a board position, and attending events hosted by the local chamber of commerce. With this rapidly expanding list of activities, Jim appeared more excited about the future.

Joyce, however, started to look concerned. "Please ensure you aren't getting too busy, though," she said. She was worried. While working, he had no time to care for himself or be fully present for their family. Now that they were in a new era, she wanted to ensure he had time to relax and spend with them. He had worked very hard over the past 40 years, and now it was time to enjoy the fruits of his labor.

That is when we did something everyone in a healthy marriage knows and loves—compromise. Part of finding a good compromise is identifying the non-negotiables, and each person's biggest priorities are different. For Jim, it was filling the work void and traveling. For Joyce, it was working a bit longer and spending time with Jim and the children.

Before they got deeper into the conversation, I covered some basic active listening principles. Active listening is the practice of being fully present in a conversation. While it sounds easy, it can take some practice to get used to it. The goal of active listening is to truly listen and focus on what the other person says. To actively listen, the participants must listen attentively without interrupting or concentrating on their own responses, making eye contact, and asking specific questions based on what the other person said. Jim and Joyce were immediately on board and dove into the conversation.

As we discussed the possibilities and options, I also followed up with questions about different aspects of their lives. How much longer did Joyce want to work? How did Jim want to fill his day-to-day time in retirement? As our time neared, Joyce said, "I would love it if we could take one or two big trips a year, one of them with our kids. I'll work for five more years, and then I will retire, too. We can downsize into a smaller home close to where Nick and Alice have landed."

This hit it out of the park for Jim. "Which place would you like to visit first?" he asked.

"Japan," said Joyce with a grin.

"Now that is a place I want to go! Maybe we can go next winter? There is so much I want to photograph there," Jim exclaimed. He continued, "Then I will only add one activity to my schedule at a time to see how much time each commitment will take. If the extracurriculars start taking up more than 25 hours a week or impacting our travel options, I will cut back."

He continued. "The first thing I want to try out is mentoring. I want to start mentoring young entrepreneurs. I received great help and advice when I was getting on my feet. I want to help the next generation get going, too."

That was the "aha moment." Jim and Joyce sat upright, leaning in, their eyes sparkling with excitement. I could tell from their body language that this future sounded right to both. They were ready!

CHAPTER 6 REVIEW

- Retirement can feel like a giant lurch. One helpful technique to bridge the transition is pinpointing what you are missing, such as mentoring others or serving a particular cause. Once you've identified what you are missing, you can find new ways to fulfill those needs.
- If you are working on retirement plans with a significant other, leverage the power of active listening by doing the following:
    - Stay present in the conversation.
    - When they are talking, don't think about your response or interrupt.
    - Orient your body towards and make eye contact with your partner.
    - Ask specific follow-up questions based on what the other person said.

CHAPTER 6 DISCUSSION QUESTIONS

1. Are you struggling with the transition to retirement? Reflect on what you miss from your career. Are there any overlapping areas or common themes?

2. Review your responses to the previous question. Identify the top two or three things that you miss. Brainstorm ways to fill those gaps in retirement.

3. Are you navigating retirement with a spouse or significant other? Are you on the same page regarding the retirement lifestyle you want? Could you better leverage active listening in your relationship?

CHAPTER 7

Unpacking Passions—What Do You Really Want from Your Retirement?

WHEN YOU DO quit work, take time to reacquaint yourself with what it means to live authentically. If you love cats, retirement can give you time to volunteer at an animal shelter. If you love baseball, you can visit a new park each year to watch your favorite team. If you love to travel, choose your most desired destinations and go.

Whatever you enjoy, there is no need to rush through everything at once! Spread out your adventures to respect your capacity. Embrace the novelty of retirement and don't feel obligated to continue doing an activity if it doesn't foster a sense of well-being and happiness.

There are some moments when you feel stuck. Sometimes, there is something you want to do, but you keep delaying. You are hesitating. Perhaps you don't know why something is holding you back from committing to pursue an interest.

When you reach these pain points, it is time to examine the underlying motivations and challenges to achieving your goals. Ask yourself, "What about the idea or hobby that I love, and what would I rather live without? Is there a better way you can achieve that aim without overtaxing your time and energy?"

One client frequently said he wanted a boat, but he kept hesitating. He had enough money to make the purchase, and we talked about it month after month. Yet, despite constantly discussing the boat, he would not buy one. Finally, after discussing the boat for 18 months, we dove deeper into the topic. "I did have a boat once," he confessed, "but it ended up being a huge pain in the neck. The maintenance, docking fees, insurance, and repairs felt like they would never end!" The upkeep and expense had driven him up the wall.

It was time to dig a little deeper so I could understand what exactly he was thinking about making this large purchase. "So, if I'm hearing you correctly, owning a boat is a huge pain in the neck, but you still want one?" I asked.

He replied, "I loved taking my friends out and hanging out on the water. Every summer, we would go fishing for hours and cruise around a few times in a nearby lake. One time, we spent hours just drinking beers and fishing out there, and my friend, Greg, got the worst sunburn I have ever seen." He started to chuckle at the memory.

This is when the light came on: the solution was not necessarily to own a boat—it was simply to spend time on a boat with his buddies. He didn't need to take on boat ownership to have a good time with his friends at the lake. A better solution we landed on was to rent a boat once a month for him and his friends. Then they could get out onto the lake and enjoy time together without the hassle of caring for a boat.

Another frequent discussion with clients that often involves feeling stuck is the idea of owning a vacation home. Many consider buying a second property only to be caught in the hassle of homeownership, with all the management and taxes accompanying it. It gets more complicated if people want to rent out their second homes when they're not being used, and suddenly use an agency or are entangled in house ownership woes, but now times two.

Some people still decide to do it despite these challenges. For them, the time, energy, and effort are well worth it to own another property. Then, they can have a home where they go to get away from everything, just how they like it.

For those who find it too bothersome or otherwise incompatible, we explore what they wanted out of a second home in the first place. Sometimes, it is more beneficial and cost-effective to write a check for $5,000 once a summer to rent a house for a month and not worry about it for the rest of the year. They have more time and energy to enjoy their vacations without worrying about additional home ownership.

CHAPTER 7 REVIEW

- Sometimes, there is something you want to do, but you procrastinate and can't move forward.
- When you are stuck in a decision, it helps to dive deeper and find the underlying issues and motivations. Brainstorm—is there another way you can achieve your aims?

CHAPTER 7 DISCUSSION QUESTIONS

1. Is there a decision on which you're stuck? If so, what is it? (If there are multiple decisions, feel free to write down all of them.) How long have you been stuck?

____

____

____

____

____

____

____

____

2. If so, why do you want to do that particular thing? Spend five minutes exploring your motivations, both the initial things that come to mind and the deeper reasons that arise after thinking about it longer. What is keeping you from achieving that goal?

3. Look at your motivations in your previous response. Are there other ways to achieve your goals besides the original scenario you listed?

4. Outline your ideal future retirement. Consider aspects such as health and well-being, community, family, home, inner growth, leisure, learning, finances, work, and major events.

5. What are your retirement non-negotiables? What do you want to prioritize?

6. What is something you have always wanted to do? Give yourself a set amount of time and brainstorm a list of things you have always wanted to try.

7. Come up with a list of activities you are willing to try, and schedule some of them so you can start.

CHAPTER 8

Beyond the Nine-to-Five—Redefining Work in Retirement

SOMETIMES, THE REVERSE can be true. Instead of worrying about overtaxing yourself, you step into retirement and realize you have too much energy that needs direction. You had all this time and energy you were expending toward your career, and now you possess an untapped energy reserve. The transition into retirement can be disconcerting in terms of energy.

Because of this, some retirees go all in and take on multiple projects. You can even choose a new career in your retirement. There is nothing wrong with choosing to work in retirement as long as you set the conditions and hold the reins. For instance, they may choose real estate for better or for worse.

Consider your history and personality if you have an abundance of energy or financial need and are contemplating work in some capacity, whether full-time or part-time. Some people cannot help but devote themselves to their careers. They find it impossible not to immerse themselves wholeheartedly in their work and quickly find themselves working 80 hours a week.

One approach I have seen work well is when clients slowly and methodically explore side careers. If they consider consulting, they might start gradually by networking to see what happens. Sometimes, they will discover a business niche waiting for them. Other times, they might realize that the consulting work doesn't match their interests.

Other retirees will explore the difference by dabbling in a few small projects without commitment. This gives them the space and time to see what works and what doesn't. It also allows them to easily cut back if they need additional time for any reason, like health, travel, or family needs. They can also add more if they find that the current mix is not enough.

This was the approach I recommended to Jim when he was considering how to reaffirm his identity in retirement. One option that he entertained was jumping into consulting. His decades of experience growing and leading a hardware store chain gave him valuable business acumen and regional and commercial knowledge. He was eager to share this knowledge in a financially beneficial way as he eased into retirement!

He started by networking at the local chamber of commerce meetings and meet-ups for new businesses. Jim found a particularly beneficial niche in consulting businesses that were opening additional locations in his region. He assisted them in identifying the best spots to open new locations, navigating local bureaucratic procedures, and transitioning from managing one business to multiple businesses at once.

The best part of his consultancy practice was that he could choose his clients and time his work based on his schedule. He never took on more than one client at a time and purposely scheduled projects so he and Joyce could go on trips together. And, if a client was too troublesome, he could finish his project and move on!

As with everything else, it is about finding the right mix. Also, remember that you (hopefully) do not need to work. This is your retirement, and the time to enjoy yourself. If it gives you energy and feels like a great use of your time, then pursuing job opportunities can be beneficial in retirement. However, if it feels like you are slipping back into the humdrum of a regular career, pause to reflect: Is this really what you want? Because before you know it, you may find yourself very busy managing everything else in retirement!

CHAPTER 8 REVIEW

- The drop-off into retirement can be disconcerting in terms of energy, income, and identity. Sometimes, retirees choose to start second careers in retirement to fill their needs.
- While there is nothing wrong with working in retirement, you must be intentional and ensure that the work benefits you.

- Two beneficial approaches to retirement careers are (1) approaching it slowly, small, and methodically, or (2) undertaking multiple smaller projects. Both of these methods allow you to maintain control of the tempo of the work.

CHAPTER 8 DISCUSSION QUESTIONS

1. Are you considering a retirement career? If so, what are your motivations? What are some areas that interest you?

2. Are you a person who can't resist committing to a full-time career? How will this phase of life differ from your career life? Are you retiring or making a career shift? If work were balanced, how would that look?

3. Develop a list of activities you are willing to try, and schedule some of those activities to start trying them out.

CHAPTER 9

Location, Location, Retirement—Find the Ideal Spot for Your Next Chapter

SUE WAS LOOKING to move in. She was done with the winter weather and wanted to relocate before the next snowfall. Before jumping into which state she should live in to reduce her tax burden or any other financial planning topic, I asked, "Do you feel like you have the capacity right now to look for a new home and move? Which areas do you feel you have the energy to work on now?"

"Staying busy actually helps," she said, "I enjoy going to open houses."

"Okay, good! Tell me this: what comes to mind when you think of home? What would that be like if you waved a magic wand and had a house you felt good about living in?" Sue described how she would like to live as close to the ocean as possible while also being near medical care.

"What do you enjoy about being near the ocean?" I asked.

"Walking on the beach with my dogs and enjoying the sunshine really helps my mood and the small beach town vibe."

She had many options for where she could live and was ready to downsize. She reemphasized that she wanted to be close to the ocean. "The ocean makes me feel peaceful and reminds me of Frank," she said. With these variables in mind, we began our search.

The best location for retirement is a personal choice that depends on individual preferences, priorities, and lifestyle goals. However, there are often many other factors to consider, including healthcare, climate, and culture. I recommend that clients take time to visit prospective locations, talk to locals, and gather as much information as possible to make an informed decision so that they find the best location that aligns with their vision for retirement.

Here are some factors to consider as you weigh different locations for retirement:

- Climate and Weather Events: Some prefer mild, year-round temperatures, while others enjoy distinct seasons. When weighing options, it may be beneficial to consider how certain climates might affect physical ailments, such as arthritis. Calculating extreme weather events for specific locales and how they may impact where you want to live is also valuable.

- Healthcare: Research the availability and quality of healthcare services in potential locations, including proximity to hospitals, clinics, and specialized medical facilities. When considering this point, remember to include access to services such as dental care. Sometimes, healthcare costs can fluctuate depending on the area you choose, which can be important to take into account.
- Proximity to Family and Friends: Being close to loved ones can provide a support system and enhance your overall well-being during retirement. If you have grandkids or are encountering health issues, you may want to be no more than a twenty-minute drive away (or even a few blocks!).
- Community and Culture: Explore communities that host cultural events, recreational opportunities, and a social scene aligned with your interests. Find out what recreational activities are available in the area. Whether you enjoy hiking, golfing, cultural events, or something else, select a location that provides more opportunities for activities you love.
- Cost of Living: From food to housing expenses, living in some areas is significantly more expensive than in others. Taxes, utilities, and more all factor into a place's total cost of living. Considering budgetary constraints, think about what is feasible as you weigh options.

Sue selected her top three locations based on criteria that interested her: Corpus Christi, Texas; Myrtle Beach, South Carolina;

and Marco Island, Florida. She had a few friends in each of these cities and was charmed by the lifestyle options they offered. She was mostly excited to be near the beach, no matter which she chose.

She planned to visit them all for two weeks throughout the coming year to scope out the areas and communities. A year after retirement, Sue visited all her top retirement locations and decided to move to a condo near the beach in Corpus Christi, where she quickly found a new lifestyle that suited her much better.

Wherever and however you decide to spend your retirement, you must make the best choice for you. Think of different components of your ideal life and prioritize what will make the most significant impact. You have worked hard for this future. How will you savor it?

CHAPTER 9 REVIEW

- Many people consider moving in retirement. Some key factors to consider include climate and weather, healthcare, proximity to friends and family, community and culture, and cost of living.
- If you are considering a significant move, identify the most important factors (e.g., proximity to the ocean and affordability) to find places you'd be interested in. Then, plan to visit those locations as you decide which is the best fit.

CHAPTER 9 DISCUSSION QUESTIONS

1. Are you considering moving? Which factors contribute primarily to your decision?

2. Write out your top list of places that meet those criteria:

3. Create a rough plan to visit those places to determine the ideal retirement spot and what you would like to learn before you go (think healthcare providers, access to transit, and things like that). Consider what time of year you want to visit each place and how long you would like to stay to determine the best fit.

____

____

____

____

____

____

____

____

CHAPTER 10

Finding a New Rhythm—Using the Two-Week Exercise to Imagine the Future

AFTER DISCUSSING SOME towns that interested her, I asked Sue what she wanted to do when the weather was bad or if she had done all the beach walking she felt she could do for a day. She sighed and said, "I don't know. Maybe watch TV?" She avoided eye contact as she said it, and her shoulders slumped.

When life is overwhelming and we're facing change, we should pause and go back to basics rather than trying to find more things to do or more changes to make. Sue needed to take care of herself and recalibrate. I asked her which things she felt would help her recharge and feel grounded again. She said she wanted to find ways to form closer friendships. Sue was also looking for a way to move more and be healthier. Her other priorities included her two dogs and finding a new place to live.

I recommended that she imagine two weeks of her ideal retirement life. How would she use her time in a fulfilling way? Were there any classes she wanted to take or new activities she wanted to try? Watching TV for a week might be okay, but not for two. How else would she occupy her time?

I particularly encouraged her to seek activities that addressed different needs and aspects of life. Could she exercise and socialize? Were there activities where she could grow internally, connect with her community, and foster learning? We brainstormed options ranging from classes to group trips to volunteer work before she left the session to work on her two-week plan at home.

She took the exercise seriously, created a schedule on a piece of paper, and brought it to our next meeting. Here is roughly what it looked like:

	Monday	Tuesday	Wednesday	Thursday	Friday	Saturday	Sunday
Week 1	Meditate Exercise Class Dog Park Groceries Beach Walk	Beach Walk Meditate Life Admin Volunteer	Meditate Exercise Class Bridge Club	Meditate Doctor's Appt	Meditate Exercise Class Dog Park	Meditate Hiking Group with Dogs	Meditate Lunch with Friend
Week 2	Meditate Exercise Class Dog Park Groceries	Meditate Life Admin Volunteer	Meditate Exercise Class Bridge Club	Meditate Dentist Appt	Meditate Exercise Class Dog Park	Meditate Hiking Group with Dogs	Meditate Lunch with Friend

Sue planned several activities for each day of the week, including exercise classes three times a week and joining a Wednesday afternoon bridge group. Not only would the former enhance her physical well-being and the latter provide learning opportunities, but both of these activities would be great for making friends! She was also looking into different dog-friendly hiking groups so she and her pups could make friends together.

The two-week exercise can fulfill another essential purpose. It can help you understand how your retirement time will be filled. It offers an opportunity to plan out activities and habits that are important to you so they don't slip away in the busyness of everyday life.

CHAPTER 10 REVIEW

- One way to find your ideal retirement life is to do the two-week exercise, which involves envisioning your life for those two weeks.
- Be specific and pragmatic as you complete the two-week exercise. Imagine what you would like to do each day and how you'll take care of yourself (e.g., health, community, etc.).

CHAPTER 10 DISCUSSION QUESTIONS

1. Complete the two-week activity:

	Monday	Tuesday	Wednesday	Thursday	Friday	Saturday	Sunday
Week 1							
Week 2							

2. Review what you have so far. Is there anything missing, such as time for appointments or an activity that aligns with one of your values?

3. Is there something to look forward to every day?

4. How is the balance of your schedule? Do you need to find more activities to occupy your time, reduce your commitments, or do you have just the right mix?

5. Do you want to establish any new habits? If so, make a plan below for establishing them.

CHAPTER 11

Index Card Method

EVEN WITH YOUR two-week calendar roughly laid out, we all know that the best-laid plans often go awry. It can be helpful to have backup activities when your plans change. For example, bad weather might keep you inside when you usually go for a walk. A favorite club might reschedule the weekly meeting. When unexpected situations pop up, the index card method can be beneficial. Here's how you do it:

1. Get an old-fashioned index card box, some index cards, a sheet of paper, and a pen.
2. Write a list of very specific activities you can do. Don't write something vague like "go out to eat." Instead, write out, "Go out to eat for dinner at Johnny's Fish Shack," or "Go to the gym and train upper body," or "Go to the library and pick out a fiction book written in the last five years."
3. Once you have a list of specific activities, write them on index cards, shuffle them, and put them in the index card box.

4. When planning your week, if the weather changes or you feel like you're in a rut, open the box, pull out a card, and do whatever is on the card.

This works well for several reasons. Firstly, you are the one who came up with the ideas, and these are things that you like or would actually do. Secondly, it is specific enough that you won't experience decision fatigue trying to determine what to do. This is why picking a restaurant is so hard—too many options! Third, you're more willing to do an activity that you permitted yourself to do in the first place and are less likely to yell at your partner for telling you to get your butt off the couch!

CHAPTER 11 REVIEW

- Even with your rough plan for how you will fill retirement, it helps to have a backup plan for when life inevitably happens. One helpful tip is to use the index card method. The method involves filling in index cards with specific activities you can do on the fly, such as going to the gym or reading a new book. Whenever you have a sudden gap in your schedule or feel like you are in a rut, you can open your index card box and try the activity on one of the index cards.
- The index card method is effective because it involves your ideas, avoids decision fatigue, and permits you to do that activity.

CHAPTER 11 ACTIVITY

1. Buy a box of index cards and write an activity on at least 10 cards (ideally more). Put the box somewhere handy where you will see it.
2. Have a test run and try out an activity. Which did you choose? How did it go?

CHAPTER 12

From Frustration to Fulfillment—Embracing New Hobbies

SUE ATTENDED YMCA classes in Corpus Christi, Texas, along with walking and Bunco groups. When I checked in with her, she still felt a bit unsatisfied. She still had too much energy and time on her hands, so she thought about adding another activity or two, one at a time, to her schedule. She didn't want to engage in anything with too high a commitment or pressure, just something to add a bit of novelty and challenge.

She considered some activities that she already loved to do, and one thing that she had always enjoyed was drawing. After making a list and checking out available local classes, she decided to try watercolor painting. Sue signed up for a class through a regional art center on Monday evenings and enjoyed the teacher and her classmates. During our next call, however, she expressed frustration about her progress and considered quitting.

The transition can be difficult when you come from a career where you were confident and knowledgeable. Suddenly, you are a beginner again. However, you have been a beginner before, and look how far you went when you invested time and energy into those new activities!

This can be difficult for people who excel at certain things. For example, it can be deeply frustrating if you are a fantastic baker and start learning to cook. Baking and cooking are related, but not the same. Similarly, Sue was very good at drawing but had not learned how to paint. They are similar and related skills, but not the same. That can be frustrating!

As you add on and try out new activities, it is crucial to give them time. You may not hit it off right away. There is a learning curve for every new activity you learn. You have to try stuff long enough to see whether it will work and whether you like it. At the end of the day, you might not like that activity, and that's fine. However, give new hobbies sufficient time for you to decide either way.

Sue eventually moved away from watercolors to explore other art media, which she enjoyed more. She was grateful for being able to explore them first and continued taking various art classes at the art center. The classes and exploration kept her learning, growing, and making many new friends.

It is also valuable to allow enough time to see results when you are diving into new social groups. It can be challenging to break into a group when you are the new person and everyone else knows each other.

CHAPTER 12 REVIEW

- Hobbies provide value in many ways, including outlets for identity, socializing, exercise, and creativity. They can supplement areas of your life where you need additional support.
- Learning new things and joining new groups can be frustrating, particularly when transitioning from an area where you were a leader and expert in your field. Give yourself grace and keep perspective as you learn new things.

CHAPTER 12 DISCUSSION QUESTIONS

1. Make a list of your current hobbies. Are there any that you're particularly passionate about? What are some hobbies that you want to explore?

2. Do you need to bolster aspects of your life (e.g., exercise, socialization, etc.)? Can any of these hobbies help you meet these other needs?

3. Are you struggling to fit into a new group related to your hobby? If so, are there skills you need to learn to bridge the gap? Should you join a group where you know more people or should you start a new one?

PART 3

What Is *Financially* Enough

SUE'S INITIAL QUESTIONS focused on whether she had sufficient *finances*. Amid her many questions, she wanted to know exactly when she should take Social Security to maximize her benefits and how she could best manage her wealth. She was concerned about her financial security and making a plan for the next few decades. Sue wanted to be sure that she was going to be okay.

As a personal financial advisor, I would be remiss if I didn't dig into finances.

After all, that is the primary reason my clients walk in the door. Finances can get complicated quickly, and they want to know what is enough financially to secure their future. There are many things to learn and consider when planning your finances, and, as we discussed in previous chapters, there are numerous factors to navigate in retirement beyond the financial basics.

However, if you already have a financial planner in place or have a good handle on your finances, skip over this section and move ahead! This chapter is here if you ever do need it.

If you want a high-level breakdown of retirement finances, this section is for you. It is not a comprehensive dive, but a starting point so you can get started in the right direction if you haven't explored this before. Many other books and resources offer a more in-depth look into retirement finances, but this workbook section will help you start.

CHAPTER 13

Creating a Comprehensive Financial Picture—Understanding Your Holdings

As Sue and I reviewed her finances, we needed to know where her money was. Sue had collected several retirement accounts, pensions, savings accounts, and other investments throughout her career. In fact, she had 14 financial accounts across five different institutions.

If you are like Sue and have many accounts that need tracking, the first step is to list them on a spreadsheet or a piece of paper. Next, identify which ones have online logins and which ones use paper statements.

If you have paper statements, gather them and create logins for those accounts for easier access and monitoring. Review your list of accounts, noting the recent account balance, the type of account, and a general description of the holdings.

Once you have this list, take a snapshot of your net worth by totaling your assets and subtracting your liabilities or debts. In Sue's case, her only debt was a small mortgage left on her house.

We then delved into the details of her holdings and savings. The key considerations are how much money is in emergency reserves, how much is set aside for short-term expenditures, and how much is invested in low, medium, or high-risk investments. We examined the performance, costs, and tax efficiency for each asset (e.g., cash, stocks, bonds, and mutual funds). Once we had all the pieces in hand, we could step back to see how they worked together as one larger machine.

Most of Sue's investments had moderate to higher than average fees. However, her investments had also gained a lot. Since changing the investments would trigger some taxes, we needed a careful plan and evaluation of whether any changes were worthwhile.

We discussed her desired mix of equities, fixed income, real estate, and alternative investments. From there, we identified redundant or overlapping investments within the portfolio and consolidated them to streamline management and reduce costs. For example, Sue decided not to hold multiple mutual funds with similar performance, so we consolidated them into a single diversified or exchange-traded fund.

We set up a new system once we had the big picture of her financial holdings. At my firm, Great Path Planning, we typically set aside a minimum of three months of living expenses at the client's local bank, plus any additional short-term expenses, like a car purchase or the costs of a renovation, so this is what we set up for Sue. She was very curious about this point, to which I explained that leaving money in the market is risky if you need the cash within a short time frame.

Even after we made a plan to reduce the number of her accounts, it was still too much. Like other clients, Sue found her finances too complex and time-consuming. Whenever my clients have either or both of these concerns, I recommend automating as much as possible—deposits, withdrawals, transfers, bill paying, and anything else that removes a financial transaction off their plate. I even established recurring transfers from her investment accounts, so it felt like she was still getting a paycheck and didn't have to think about it.

Sue was surprised by how much time and peace of mind that move had created!

Start financial planning with small steps that you can take immediately. For example, start by automating some of the bills you pay or how you receive your statements. If you need help to do these things, find resources and people who can help you. Another suggestion is to start by writing down your account information so people can access it in an emergency. Alternatively, choose a specific day each month to log into your accounts so you can see how much money you have and feel reassured without constantly checking.

Earmarking is another strategy that can help meet financial targets. It involves setting aside cash in a money market for a significant expense like a home renovation or taxes. The key is to be flexible with earmarked funds. Feel free to reinvest the money if the fund is no longer necessary.

CHAPTER 13 REVIEW

- For a clear picture of your financial holdings:
    - List your accounts on a spreadsheet or a piece of paper.
    - Mark those that have online logins or that still operate with paper statements.
    - Collect paper statements and logins for easier access and monitoring.
    - Annotate a recent account balance, account type, and general holding description.
    - Calculate your net worth by summing assets (e.g., stocks, cash, fully-owned property, etc.) and subtracting liabilities/debts (e.g., credit card debt, mortgage, medical debt, etc.).
- Dig into the details of your holdings and savings, including the amounts in emergency reserves, short-term expenditures, and low, medium, or high-risk investments.
- Consider your ideal mix of equities, fixed-income, real estate, and alternative investments to achieve your goals (minimizing risk or leaving an estate for heirs).
- Consolidate redundant or overlapping investments in your portfolio to streamline management and reduce costs. Automate as much as possible, including deposits,

withdrawals, transfers, bill payments, and any other financial transactions you handle.

- Set aside at least three months of living expenses for an emergency fund plus any additional short-term expenses, like a car purchase or renovation costs.

CHAPTER 13 DISCUSSION QUESTIONS

1. Think about life as covered in previous parts. What does life look like now, and how might it change?

____

____

____

____

____

____

____

____

____

2. What does it cost to live today, and how might that change?

____

____

____

____

____

3. Activity: Your Financial Holdings

    - Calculate your net worth and holdings in all of your individual accounts using the steps identified in the chapter to get a clear picture of your financial holdings at the highest level.
        - Estimated net worth: _______
    - How do your different accounts compare in performance (e.g., gain)? What do you receive in exchange for lower-priced accounts (e.g., lower risk)?

- Highlight redundant accounts. Can you consolidate them for easier management, or are there downsides, such as taxes, to consider?

____

____

____

____

____

____

____

____

____

- With another color, highlight accounts you are unsure how to access. On your calendar, set a time and date to start working through the issues with customer support. If you receive paper statements, make an online login and explore ways to automate your account for greater ease.

CHAPTER 14

Crunching the Numbers—Understanding Monthly Expenditures

AFTER WE HAD clarified Sue's holdings, we discussed her monthly and annual expenditures and how much she usually spent. To start, we looked at her bank checking statements and calculated how much money she usually spent per statement. As long as a person completely pays their credit card bills every month, like Sue did, this is an effective way to get a quick estimate of their monthly spending.

We reviewed the bank account statement and calculated the average amount left each month. After identifying the cause, we excluded a month or two with exceptionally high withdrawals above the average. It is often the month of vacation or the month you pay for an annual or semiannual insurance or tax bill that causes the deviation. For simplicity's sake, we averaged in any consistently recurring costs. We left out any one-time expenses, like a once-in-a-lifetime trip to Europe (for now).

We added up these amounts to see how much she needed to live comfortably every month. It ended up being about $7,000 a month for her to continue living her current lifestyle.

We then considered the changes she was contemplating—moving to a new home and taking more yoga classes. We researched the cost-of-living difference to be near the beach and incorporated those costs into the monthly budget, and adjusted it for the sale of her home in New York. The results showed that living in New York would be the same as living at the beach!

One thing I noticed: Sue left medical expenses off her budget. As a partner at a law firm, she had a very generous health insurance plan with reimbursement for out-of-pocket costs. I adjusted her budget to include Medicare, a supplemental plan, and out-of-pocket expenses. She also added that she would like to lease a car, which would also adjust her expenses. We landed at an average monthly number of $8,000 per month after income taxes.

CHAPTER 14 REVIEW

- Look at your checking statements and see how much you usually spend per statement. This is an effective way to get a quick estimate of your monthly spending, provided you pay off your credit card bills completely every month.

  - Stick to recurring costs. Set aside months with very high withdrawals, but note the cause.
- The average monthly costs are a monthly estimate of how much you'll need to live comfortably.
- If any changes are coming up, such as healthcare, or if you are considering a move, research and estimate the impact on your cost of living.

CHAPTER 14 DISCUSSION QUESTIONS

1. Estimate your monthly spending. A quick way is to total a year of spending and then divide by 12.

   Estimated monthly spending = __________

   - Note any upcoming financial changes, such as moving to a different area.

____

____

____

____

____

____

____

____

____

____

CHAPTER 15

Introducing the 4% Rule—A Retirement Withdrawal Guideline

WITH A ROUGH idea of her monthly spending, I began discussing the 4% rule with Sue. The 4% rule, created by William Bengen in 1994, states that retirees can withdraw 4% of their savings in the first year of retirement and then continue to withdraw the same amount (adjusted for inflation) in subsequent years, provided they have saved a sufficient amount.[1]

If their retirement funds are evenly divided between stocks and bonds, they can have a 30-year retirement without running out of money. For example, if a retiree saved $5 million, which was split between stocks and bonds, then the retiree could safely withdraw about $200,000 per year for 30 years.

1 William P. Bengen, "Determining Withdrawal Rates Using Historical Data," *Journal of Financial Planning*, October 1994, 171–80, https://kyestates.com/wp-content/uploads/2015/02/Bengen1.pdf.

The 4% rule provides a helpful starting point for discussing how much clients can comfortably withdraw. I don't strictly follow it. Many factors, such as their intended legacy funds, can influence the exact withdrawal rate for a particular client. However, this guide offers a quick, simple, and generally effective way to consider retirement withdrawals.

I did this with Sue, who had a total portfolio of $4 million. Based on this principle, she could withdraw about $160,000 per year.

"This is just a ballpark figure to start. We'll jump into the nitty gritty here soon," I told her. "But do you think you could live comfortably on that?"

"Absolutely!" she said as her shoulders eased in relief. "I think so anyway."

CHAPTER 15 REVIEW

- The 4% rule states that retirees can withdraw 4% of their savings in the first year of retirement and continue to withdraw that amount (adjusted for inflation) in subsequent years, provided they have saved a sufficient amount.[2]
- If their retirement funds are evenly split between stocks and bonds, they will be able to have a 30-year retirement without depleting their finances.

---

2 Bengen, "Determining Withdrawal Rates."

CHAPTER 15 DISCUSSION QUESTIONS

1. Take your financial holdings total from Chapter 13, and multiply it by 0.04 to find your 4% rule number:

   ____

2. Compare this figure to your average monthly spending in Chapter 14. Do you currently spend more or less than the 4% rule?

CHAPTER 16

Calculating Monthly Needs—Timing Social Security Withdrawals by Month

I THEN TURNED to one of her major questions: when should she take Social Security?

I drew the following chart using her monthly living expenses, taxes, and key points she could draw from Social Security.

Figure 16.1

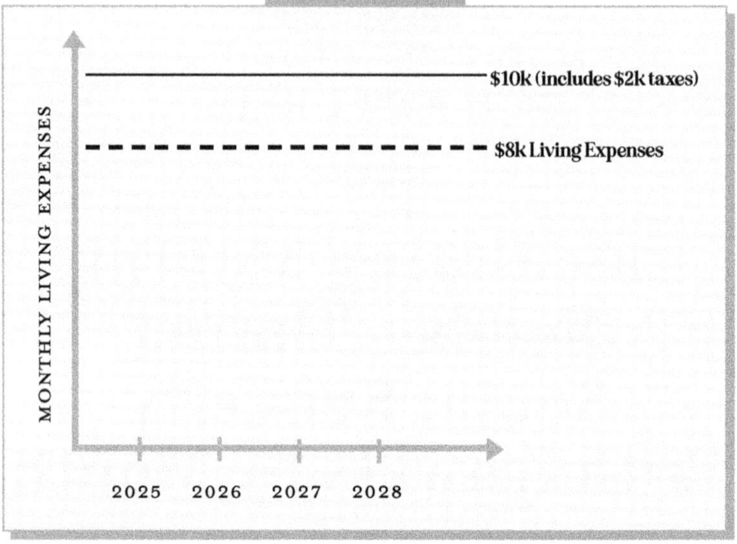

This chart shows monthly living expenses. Based on the spending estimate we created, Sue would need to receive $8,000 each month. We can't forget about Uncle Sam, so I added another $2,000 per month for taxes, bringing the monthly total to $10,000. According to this rough estimate, we would transfer $10,000 from her portfolio on the fifth of each month.

I then started to show what it would look like if she turned on Social Security at different ages. We examined the monthly gap between her income and her desired spending. In this case, there is a $10,000 a month gap for the next two years, then she could turn on Social Security early with a $7,500 a month gap moving forward. Or, she could wait five years and then maintain a $4,000 monthly gap in her steady state. Regardless, we would help manage the gap, as it would be withdrawn monthly from the portfolio and transferred to checking accounts so Sue could spend it.

The difference between claiming Social Security early or later in Sue's case was her anticipated longevity. There is a breakeven point; the longer you wait to receive Social Security, the more you get per month. However, you forgo payment for several years to obtain that extra benefit. For many people, the breakeven point occurs after 78 years old.

Sue was committed to living a healthy lifestyle, but both of her parents had died from health-related causes in their early 70s. They hadn't been as health-conscious as her, but it was still important to consider.

At the forefront of their minds was money. They spent decades stashing away the money needed for their retirement, and here it was—at least for Jim. They both came from scrappy backgrounds. Both sets of parents were shaped by the Depression and World War II, and their parents were extremely thrifty. Both Jim and Joyce grew up in families where they patched their clothes and always shopped on clearance.

Their similar childhoods shaped how they managed things while starting their own family. Jim and Joyce refurbished their furniture, made house repairs and upgrades, clipped coupons, and closely budgeted for years. Most of all, they worked hard. Jim frequently worked 70-hour weeks to stay ahead of the competition and build his businesses. They knew the value of hard work and a dollar.

They were grappling with the big change ahead of them. They were well-prepared for a comfortable retirement after selling Jim's business and taking stock of their investments. Still, it made them feel uneasy. What would it be like to spend money instead of making it? Would there be enough?

I went through a similar process with Jim and Joyce when they asked me about Social Security. We estimated their monthly spending, looked at their holdings, applied the 4% rule to start, and then began to consider how things might look depending on when they began withdrawing Social Security.

Based on the 4% rule, they could also expect to withdraw $8,000 per month. Once again, I added $2,000 per month to create a tax buffer, and then we started to examine the different phases of withdrawals between the two of them.

Since no one knows when they will die in advance, one spouse often delays their claim while the other takes it earlier.

One key point in our discussion was that Jim had been the primary income earner between them, considering his business success and Joyce's years as a stay-at-home mother. Another key point was that Joyce was still in the workforce, even though she planned to retire in a few years.

We looked at their steady-state monthly income and assessed what it would look like if Jim started withdrawing Social Security early. However, I urged them to consider waiting to withdraw Jim's Social Security until it was at maximum benefit. Since Jim was the primary earner in their relationship, they would benefit if they waited to withdraw his Social Security. This was also true if he passed away first. In the event of his passing, Joyce would receive an additional payment from the government so that she would receive the same as his withdrawals.

CHAPTER 16 REVIEW

- To best understand when to withdraw Social Security, it helps to create a chart showing your estimated monthly expenses plus taxes. Then, pencil in a few potential milestones for Social Security and how much you'd receive moving forward. This will include when you can first receive Social Security and when you would maximize your Social Security withdrawal.
- Observe the difference in your monthly withdrawals based on the differing Social Security payments.
- Decide what makes the most sense in your situation based on whether you believe you will live for a short, medium, or long amount of time.
- Couples can choose to balance the two by having the spouses start withdrawals at different points (e.g., one spouse starts taking withdrawals at first availability and the other withdraws at maximum benefit).

CHAPTER 16 DISCUSSION QUESTIONS

1. Activity: Try making the monthly spending graphs like I created previously in the chapter. Examine your monthly spending to see the average gap in spending every month and year.

- If you are deciding when to withdraw Social Security, plot different withdrawals to see how they impact your monthly gaps over time.

If you are married and deciding when to start Social Security withdrawals with your spouse, how can you two stagger withdrawals for maximum benefit?

Figure 16.2

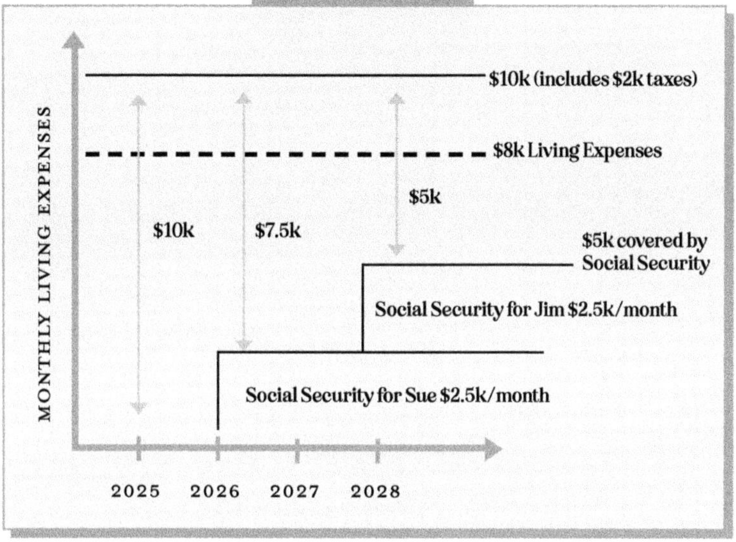

Figure 16.3

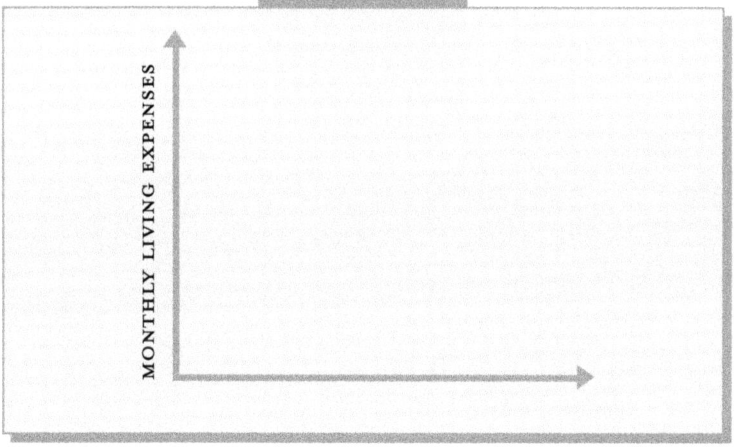

CHAPTER 17

Calculating Annual Needs—Timing Social Security Withdrawals by Year and Including Major Financial Events

THESE MONTHLY CALCULATIONS were only one part of the picture. We needed to factor in more details to determine the best time for Sue to withdraw Social Security. In particular, I needed to know about any major financial events she was planning and their associated costs.

Major events can be a lot of different things. They can include significant trips, planned major surgeries, and big purchases like buying a new car. Major financial events also include any other major purchases on the horizon, such as funding graduate school for your grandchildren. In Sue's case, she wanted to sell her current house and buy a new one in another city. Before selling her home, she would likely want to upgrade the kitchen and bathrooms, which would be another major event.

I asked her how much she would spend on renovations. She shifted slightly in her chair before saying, "I'm not sure. How much does it cost to renovate a kitchen these days?"

Before making a long-term plan, it is essential to know approximately how much the major purchases cost. This will likely involve obtaining a series of quotes or rudimentary searches to understand the price of various items and services. To estimate the kitchen and bathroom renovation costs, she created a list of renovation projects for each room and provided contact information for a reputable local contractor that could provide initial quotes. We hopped on Zillow and looked at condos and houses in the areas where she wanted to move.

When she returned to my office the following week, she had a rough idea of the cost of each of these major events.

It can be overwhelming to face a list of large purchases or tasks. This often results in analysis paralysis, making you feel frozen by the things left to figure out. In these situations, one of the most helpful things to do is create a detailed list of the figures and information you need. Then, set a specific day or time to call for the quotes you need to start making your budget. Small steps in the right direction make all the difference!

CHAPTER 17 REVIEW

- To create your long-term financial plan, you need estimates of upcoming major events such as renovations, trips, and other large financial commitments.
- When you feel overwhelmed by creating estimates for large events, break them into smaller pieces. Make a detailed list of what you need to know and places to contact for quotes. Set aside a day and time to begin gathering the necessary quotes.

CHAPTER 17 DISCUSSION QUESTIONS

1. What major events do you have planned for the next 5 to 10 years? Make a list of every significant major financial event that you need or would like below.

2. Next to the major financial events listed above, write a rough estimate of how much they will cost. If you are unsure, write a plan below for how you will create a rough estimate for each item. Schedule a time on your calendar for you to execute that plan.

CHAPTER 18

Calculating Annual Needs—Timing Social Security Withdrawals by Year

ONCE WE HAD the estimates for Sue's major financial events, we could start examining what it would be like to withdraw Social Security on an annual basis and how that would affect her finances. I drew the following chart to show her how it would look.

Figure 18.1

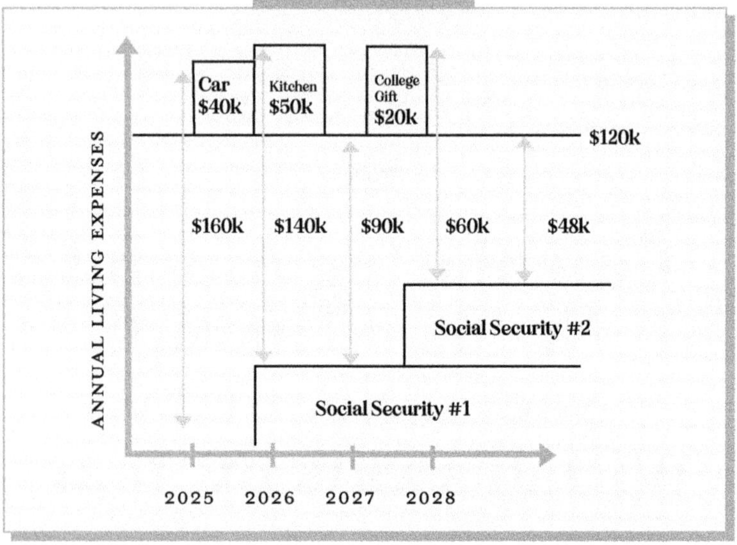

I took the upper estimate from the monthly chart—$10,000 a month—and multiplied it by 12 for an annual basic expenditure estimate. I added the big expenditures planned for the given years (the kitchen and bathroom renovations) to the upcoming year, and then an estimate for her moving costs and house costs to the year after that.

I calculated the gap and the annual amount we needed to withdraw from investments and savings to do everything Sue wanted to do. Sue had a large gap for the first few years as she renovated and moved, but the gap lessened substantially after that.

We reassessed how Social Security would help meet her needs based on when she started withdrawing. If she began taking a partial withdrawal earlier at age 62, her steady-state average gap would be $90,000 a year after she began withdrawing. If she waited until she was 67 before she began withdrawing, her gap would shrink to $60,000 a year.

We began discussing a difficult yet important topic: how long did Sue think she would live? A short, medium, or long time? Sue thought about it for a moment. "Well, my mother lived until she was 92, but my father passed away at 68. I think I'll be somewhere in between."

It is impossible to know precisely when to start withdrawing Social Security to optimize their benefits unless they have a crystal ball or some form of foresight that allows them to know when they will die. In lieu of precise knowledge, we must make our best guesses and adjust the sails as we go. What is your family history like, and how are your habits?

Most people expect to live a moderate amount of time and adjust their finances accordingly. Sometimes, life and health events compel them to make significant changes earlier than planned. Other times, they live much longer than they anticipated.

You can create this chart on your own to see how it will look. I have software that does all this fancy stuff and can make far more detailed versions of these charts. However, it can become confusing quickly. It is challenging to know which underlying variables factor into this software and similar programs, making it hard to understand exactly what they convey. Suddenly, it is a deep and technical conversation.

I enjoy creating these charts so people can see how it will look at different times and with varying withdrawals. I then use professional-grade software to double-check our work and provide more details to ensure we're not missing anything like tax rates. It does the number crunching to get a clearer picture before we wander into the weeds.

CHAPTER 18 REVIEW

- After you create your monthly chart and have rough estimates for major expenditures, create an annual chart to determine the best time to start your Social Security withdrawals.
    - The annual chart should display years on the y-axis and money spent on the x-axis. Establish a baseline of anticipated yearly expenditures based on the high-level monthly estimate created previously, multiplied by 12.
    - Add the major expenditure estimates to the years you anticipate these expenditures occurring.
    - Pencil in start dates for withdrawing Social Security and the gap between what you anticipate spending versus what you would receive from Social Security, depending on when you withdraw.

CHAPTER 18 DISCUSSION QUESTIONS

1. Try your hand at creating the annual spending graph like the one I made in this chapter. Use the chart to find the average gap in spending per year.

- If you are deciding when to withdraw Social Security, plot different withdrawals to see how they impact your annual gap over time.

Figure 18.2

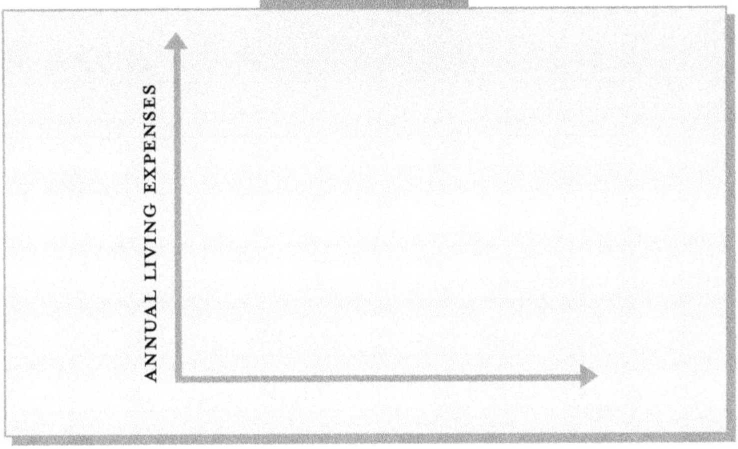

2. How does the annual gap compare to your assets? Are you overspending, or is there more wiggle room in your budget that you aren't utilizing?

3. Consider your situation, background, and family history. How does that influence your decision to start withdrawing Social Security?

CHAPTER 19

Social Security in Summary—Weighing Pros and Cons

AS PREVIOUSLY MENTIONED, it is impossible to always know when the optimum time is to withdraw Social Security, but you will be okay! If you know the underlying principle, you can go from applying numbers to applying knowledge and understanding.

As you weigh your options, be aware that your expenses will change over time. First, you will pay for health insurance, and then switch to Medicare, which is cheaper. You may start out in retirement traveling frequently, but then reduce it as health demands shift. Toward the end of life, costs usually rise for people once again. Along the way, any number of things may happen that shift your spending.

Monitoring your cash flow and holdings when deciding when to turn on Social Security is beneficial. For example, if the market crashes, it may be time to start withdrawing to relieve the withdrawal pressure from your accounts. If things go better than anticipated, perhaps waiting longer to withdraw Social Security makes more sense.

As you make these decisions with an eye on your situation, don't forget to put logic to work for you. Keeping a smartly diversified portfolio can give you the best chance for good things to happen. By doing so, you'll minimize risk and the possibility that any adverse events will have too much of an impact on you.

Another important thing to remember is that stress reduction and simplification might be more beneficial than the technical definition of financial maximization. After all, you have already made it to retirement. The goal now is to feel like it's enough, like you have a plan, and that you know the plan's implications.

Finally, you will not know the exact outcome. There will always be pros and cons as well as trade-offs. Focus on your goal and then apply wisdom to the situation. There are various options, and you must pick one in advance without knowing the outcome.

CHAPTER 19 REVIEW

- It's impossible to know the precise best time to withdraw Social Security. That would require a crystal ball. Use the charts and reasoning outlined in the previous chapters to determine what point will probably be the best.

- Your expenses will change over time. Health insurance, travel spending, care needs, and more will fluctuate and evolve over time.
- Respond to your cash flow and holdings when deciding when to turn on Social Security. For example, if the market crashes, it might be a suitable time to turn on Social Security instead of relying too heavily on your investments.
- Reduce risk, keep your portfolio diversified.
- Simplicity and minimizing stress may be better goals than financial maximization.

CHAPTER 19 DISCUSSION QUESTIONS

1. Based on the exercises from the previous sections, when do you want to start withdrawing Social Security? What are some conditions that would change that estimate?

CHAPTER 20

Other Common Retirement Finance Terms and Concepts

MANY BOOKS, VIDEOS, and other resources explore the particulars of retirement financial planning. As previously discussed, seeking assistance from a certified financial planner can ease anxiety, improve your returns, and increase your understanding. Whether you decide to DIY or seek professional assistance, here are a few more topics I am frequently asked about.

20.1 EMERGENCY FUNDS

An emergency fund should be an amount that you'll have in a savings account for any of life's unexpected major expenses to allow you to continue to thrive. Generally, the emergency funds meet deductibles for retirees for insurance claims, often related to home damage or an expensive medical procedure like surgery.

Emergency funds are vital, but it is also important not to have too much in them. Excessive funds in your emergency savings mean missing out on significant interest earnings. It can also result in losing money to inflation over the long term. Many other expenses are predictable, so we don't have to have enormous emergency reserves.

For instance, buying a car to replace a 15-year-old vehicle is generally not an emergency. You know your car is aging, and you can bake it into your financial and withdrawal plans to have funds available from your investments to cover the car purchase, assuming you do not want to lease or finance the purchase.

If we know a car purchase is coming up, but don't have a set date (within a few years, let's say), we'll often put those funds in a safer investment where the odds of losing principal are lower. The more certain we are that the car purchase is coming up, the safer the funds should be.

All your other investments should be positioned in a way that flows money to you every month for you to live on. Additionally, constructing the investments so that if there is a much larger emergency or an earlier replacement of a vehicle, we can pull money without worrying about when the market is up or down.

I recommend that clients generally plan on saving about three months' spending in an emergency fund. This helps fill the gap between some more expensive months (like the month you pay for your annual vacation) and helps people not feel "investment-rich and cash-poor." I've had clients with millions of dollars but no cash and feel poor. Sufficient wiggle room in a savings account often helps alleviate this feeling.

20.2 ANNUITIES

First, let me say there are as many particular types of annuities as there are flavors of ice cream. Different flavors of annuities go in and out of style over time, and insurance companies, which are the purveyors of annuity contracts, change their product offerings and terms over time.

One of the most common annuities to consider in retirement is a single premium immediate annuity, sometimes referred to as an SPIA. An SPIA is a contract in which a person invests a fixed amount with an insurance company and then receives payments back at a rate guaranteed by the insurance company.

Annuities provide a guaranteed income stream for a fixed period or for life. This can offer financial security, particularly in retirement, ensuring a steady flow of funds regardless of market fluctuations.

SPIAs, however, are fixed-income plans that usually involve tying up your money for an extended period, if not for the rest of your life. This can present difficulties if there is a sudden large expense.

The main attractive element of an SPIA is a fixed, predictable income stream that often pays out slightly higher than a similar portfolio of bonds. The reason this happens is due to mortality credits. This insurance term describes that some people will die early when receiving the income stream from the annuity, while others will live longer. Eliminating the liability to the deceased annuitants frees up money to be paid toward others who have survived. So it spreads the risk of dying too soon or living too long amongst a group of people rather than just one person as an individual. This can result in a positive outcome for clients who live a moderate to more extended period than other annuitants.

Fixed indexed annuities are different—they provide some fixed guarantees of growth on principal and are designed to be a vehicle for accumulating or growing wealth for some time before being taken as an income stream later. The returns can be tied to the stock market, but they protect against losses. Since there is no free lunch, the upside of growth is usually capped. This type of annuity can be helpful for people who want their money to grow more, but have a low tolerance for losses and risk.

While this sounds too good to be true, it isn't. There are restrictions and fees within the fixed indexed annuity. The devil is in the details. If the limits are appropriate for when you need to withdraw money, and if the fees aren't so high that investment returns are diminished to what you could get from a savings account, then the guarantees can be beneficial for clients who are too nervous to invest without guarantees.

Variable annuities come in many different flavors. They typically combine some insurance company guarantees with more upside and more downside. These annuities can be complicated, so careful consideration is needed before purchasing.

The main points of consideration when evaluating annuities:

1. When do you need the money, and do the withdrawal terms of the contract match the dollar amount you will need and the timing of when you need it?
2. How much are you paying in fees for the contract's guarantees and underlying investment vehicles?
3. If plans change and you need to leave, what are your options? Do you have other resources you can tap to avoid being backed into a corner?

People often ask how annuities compare with investing. The most significant advantage to investing is the *potential* for a higher rate of return than the guarantees provided by the annuity. This is especially true over more extended periods. Investing also offers greater liquidity and flexibility. Because annuities are an insurance contract, you get locked into terms that may not age well. Investments, however, offer you the ability to adjust based on strategy, market volatility, and personal circumstances. Many annuities won't allow you to draw additional funds if a considerable expense arises, but most investments will.

Another aspect to consider is that while annuities are a predictable source of income, you need to adjust for inflation. If inflation rises 2% per year, your annuity will have 20% less purchasing power in 10 years, even less when you account for the compounding effect of inflation! This can significantly impact your budget.

Like much financial planning, different instruments will help you depending on your situation. If you are stuck at one of these decisions, it can be helpful to reach out to a licensed financial planning professional, preferably one who is not selling financial products like annuities, for additional perspective.

20.3 PENSION BUYOUTS

Pension buyouts can be a polarizing subject in retirement planning. They happen when a pension is dissolved or terminated. Companies bear the burden of maintaining pension funds, and they can become quite expensive, particularly in times of bad investment performance like the dot-com bubble or the global financial crisis.

Often, pension buyouts offer two options: lump-sum cash or fixed monthly payments. Some people prefer annuities for their dependability, while others say that anybody who doesn't take a buyout and invest it in the stock market is a fool. This high-stakes decision can create reasonable feelings of anxiety for my clients who are facing this conundrum.

Consider inflation's impact on your annuity payments. If a retiree takes a buyout as an annuity at age 55, by age 85, the pension annuity may only have half the purchasing power because of inflation that it did when they first retired.

When evaluating the decision, we compare the monthly payment offered by the annuity option to the value of the lump sum. We also compare that to the client's other income sources, like other pensions, Social Security, and annuities, and their overall investment portfolio. The integration into the client's personal circumstances is more meaningful than the actuarial calculation of the present value of the annuity.

This is often not a discussion about maximizing returns but assessing risk—would you prefer to bear the investment risk and be responsible for providing yourself with a consistent stream of income from the pension buyout, or would you like to rely on the company that controls the pension to live up to their legal and financial obligation to provide the fixed monthly payments?

20.4 LIFE INSURANCE: TERM AND PERMANENT

There are generally two types of life insurance: term and permanent. Term life insurance has set beginning and ending dates and is best used to cover goals with definite endpoints. For example, if a person had young children and needed to cover caretaking duties before their passing, term insurance would be the answer because the children would likely be able to care for themselves when they become adults and get a job.

Term insurance usually benefits people with young families, for this reason, but it isn't likely to serve goals in retirement. One exception is pension replacement. If a pension doesn't have a survivor benefit or if the survivor benefit is so small that you need extra money to cover the gap, term insurance combined with an investment portfolio that you already have can be the solution. The term insurance can cover you until the investments have grown enough to fill the gap.

Suppose there is a goal without an endpoint, such as an income gap goal for which you don't have or want to set aside investments, or a legacy purpose like leaving money to a charity, to pay taxes, or to give a person a certain amount of money. In that case, permanent life insurance is the solution.

For example, permanent life insurance is an answer if you want pension replacement money forever. Also, since pensions typically do not pass on to adult children, some people will use life insurance as a proxy for the value of the pension that will stop. Their heirs receive the life insurance money since the pension money goes away and is not inheritable.

20.5 LONG-TERM CARE INSURANCE

Medical expenses balloon rapidly, particularly when mobility is impaired and if you need around-the-clock monitoring for safety and basic needs. In the U.S., the average monthly cost of care for a nursing home is $9,197 for a semiprivate room or $10,326 for a private room. In the northeastern U.S., where I and many of my clients live, we expect to pay around $12,000 to $13,000 monthly for long-term care services when needed.[3]

There are four ways to pay for long-term care services: (1) your assets, (2) long-term care insurance, (3) Medicaid (if you are impoverished), or (4) a combination. Considering long-term care insurance (LTCI) as a retiree is worthwhile. LTCI is a type of insurance that provides coverage for long-term care services like nursing homes, assisted living, or in-home care. While Medicare

3 Jeremy Clerc, "Nursing Home Costs: A State-by-State Guide," *Assisted Living Magazine*, May 8, 2025, https://assistedlivingmagazine.com/nursing-home-costs-a-state-by-state-guide.

offers some coverage for short-term medical conditions, the program doesn't cover long-term care needs.

LTCI helps cover the associated costs and offers peace of mind for yourself and your family. Many people are gun-shy about getting policies since LTCI premiums can change over time. The premiums experienced rapid increases in the past two decades because of chronic underpricing during the 1990s and early 2000s.

I discussed LTCI with Jim and Joyce. I drafted financial plans for what would happen if one of them were in a nursing home and the other was still healthy and maintaining an independent household. I also outlined what it would look like if both were in a long-term care facility or needed round-the-clock aides at home. We compared these projections to their assets and found that LTCI was necessary.

Some people can do without insurance under many everyday, average financial scenarios. But they must know if things don't go well, they are bearing the risk that they could spend more of their assets than anticipated on long-term care.

20.6 TAXES NOW OR LATER—MANAGING TAX BRACKETS USING ROTH CONVERSIONS

Traditional IRAs and 401(k)s require withdrawals when the account holders reach a certain age. These Required Minimum Distributions (RMDs) begin at age 73 for some and 75 for others.[4] The longer you wait, the more your IRA investments compound,

4 "Retirement Plan and IRA Required Minimum Distributions FAQs," IRS.gov, last updated May 27, 2025, https://www.irs.gov/retirement-plans/retirement-plan-and-ira-required-minimum-distributions-faqs.

so your account values can be tremendous. RMDs are based on your age and account value, so the older you are and the larger the account, the more you must withdraw.

For people with large RMDs and other incomes such as Social Security, investments, and pensions, the old adage of "I'll be in a lower tax bracket when I retire" is only partially true. You are probably in a lower tax bracket for part of your retirement, but with all of these incomes and forced withdrawals, you may match or exceed the tax bracket at which you put the money into the IRA or 401(k) in the first place!

To address this, we see what years tend to have high or low tax brackets and choose to either withdraw from the IRA or do a Roth Conversion. A Roth Conversion allows you to transform funds from your Traditional IRA into a Roth IRA. In this transaction, you pay taxes on the amount converted instead of paying taxes on the principal and the growth of these funds in the future. The funds have to be untouched for five years in the Roth IRA and are then available for tax-free withdrawal.

This will help to even out your taxes over the long term and can relieve tax burdens on heirs who have to pay taxes on inherited Traditional IRAs as income.

20.7 STOCK ALLOCATION SELECTION

If you receive a large sum of money all at once, like an inheritance or from the sale of your company, it's essential to develop a sensible allocation selection strategy.

You don't want to put money in various places without reasoning. I've seen people sell their business for millions of dollars and throw it into many accounts without a purpose. They buy a second house, buy a home for their kids, and spread money into gold, bonds, and specific stocks based on whatever buzz they hear. Then, they keep an unfathomable amount of cash in the bank, some even as much as $500,000, as an emergency fund. For most people, half a million dollars as an emergency fund is unnecessary. There was never a point in their life before this, and there is unlikely to be anything in the future that would lead to this kind of emergency. The one exception is experimental medical treatments not covered by insurance. This is pretty rare, so planning for it is usually superfluous.

When you determine what drives your asset allocation, you can select different areas where you'll want money. For example, you could allocate your money 60% in stocks and 40% in bonds. Looking at the historical performance of a similar portfolio over time, including when the market dips, will help you mentally prepare for the rate of return you get, what a good year looks like, and what a bad year looks like. Knowing how long things are "underwater" when the market drops is also beneficial. How long, on average, does it take to recover?

During the global financial crisis of 2008, many portfolios with a 60/40 stock-bond allocation dipped approximately 30% over about 18 months, and it took about two years after the market stopped dropping to get back to break even for people who were not withdrawing funds from their investments.[5] If someone were pulling money out of their portfolios at that time and living off their investments, it would take about five years for their portfolios to grow back to pre-crisis level. After that, there was growth again. That was one of the worst-case scenarios, so gauging how things might go is helpful.

Historically, stocks have provided higher long-term returns than other asset classes such as bonds or cash equivalents. Investing in stocks can offer retirees the potential for capital appreciation and long-term growth of their investment portfolio, helping to preserve and increase their wealth over time. However, stocks have drawbacks such as volatility, market uncertainty, dividend fluctuations, company-specific risks, and liquidity concerns.

You might want to play it overly safe because of the possible downsides of owning stocks so much that you want to put all your money in bonds. If that's the case, consider your options carefully. Suppose there is inflation, such as that experienced in the 1970s and 1980s and during the COVID-19 pandemic. In that case, bonds can experience higher levels of volatility than many bond investors are used to in the interim periods.

Instead of doing something drastic like putting all your money in bonds, gold, cash, or your mattress, devise a strategy that mentally prepares you for the market downturns and spreads the money across multiple asset types. I've observed that it isn't diversified adequately if you don't have something to complain about in your portfolio.

---

5 Ben Carlson, "The Worst Years Ever For a 60/40 Portfolio," A Wealth of Common Sense, June 5, 2022, https://awealthofcommonsense.com/2022/06/the-worst-years-ever-for-a-60-40-portfolio/.

20.8 BONDS

Bonds provide a predictable income stream through interest payments, which appeals to retirees who need a stable cash flow to cover living expenses. With a bond, you loan money to a company or a country, which they then pay back with interest. You have a legal contract with the bond issuer to pay you back with predefined terms. Bonds are generally less volatile than stocks and offer greater capital preservation and protection, which is essential for retirees who look to safeguard their wealth and minimize risk during retirement. Including bonds in an investment portfolio enhances diversification and reduces overall portfolio risk.

While bonds offer advantages such as income stability, capital preservation, and diversification for retirees with a substantial investment portfolio, they also come with drawbacks. These downsides include generally lower long-term returns than stocks, being locked into rates when interest rates may rise, and not staying ahead of rapid inflation.

CHAPTER 20 REVIEW

- Emergency fund: An amount in a savings account for any unexpected major expenses.
- Annuities: A contract providing a guaranteed income stream for a fixed period or for life. There are many types of annuities, including the following:
    - A single premium immediate annuity (SPIA) is a contract in which one invests a fixed amount with an insurance company and receives payments back at a guaranteed rate. These contracts usually involve tying

    up money for an extended period, if not the rest of one's life, and present difficulties if there is a sudden large expense.
  - Fixed-indexed annuities: Provide some fixed guarantees of growth on principal and are designed to accumulate or grow wealth for some time before being taken as an income stream later. The returns can be tied to the stock market while protecting against losses. The upside growth is usually capped. This type of annuity can be helpful for people who want their money to grow more but have a low tolerance for losses and risk.
  - Variable annuities: A blend of some guarantees from the insurance company. These annuities can be extremely complicated. Carefully consider this option before purchasing.
- Pension buyouts: Payment offered when a pension is dissolved or terminated, usually lump-sum cash or fixed monthly payments as an annuity.
  - Compare the monthly payment offered by the annuity and the value of the lump sum offered. Consider your other income sources, such as pensions, Social Security, annuities, and your overall investment portfolio. Focus on the risk you are ready to take on.
- Long-term care is costly and averages $10,000 a month for nursing home care in the U.S. There are four ways to pay for long-term care services: (1) your assets, (2) long-term care insurance (LTCI), (3) Medicaid (if impoverished), or (4) a combination of these options. LTCI covers long-term care services like nursing homes, assisted living, or

in-home care. Carefully consider your assets and the risk before forgoing LTCI.

- Roth conversions: A process to convert traditional IRAs or 401(k)s to Roth IRAs. This can help even out tax obligations if you have too much income stemming from IRA/401(k) required minimum distributions. Roth conversions can ease long-term tax burdens and the tax burden for heirs.
- Bond: A loan to a company or country, paid back with predefined terms. Bonds are a valuable asset in an investment portfolio, especially when trying to minimize risk.

CHAPTER 20 DISCUSSION QUESTIONS

1. How much is currently in your emergency savings? ____________
2. How many months would that sustain you if necessary? ____________
3. Are you considering a pension buyout? If so, how are you weighing your options?

____
____
____
____
____
____
____

4. Do you have long-term care insurance? If not, why not?

5. Are you considering Roth conversions? What are some factors that are influencing your decision?

CHAPTER 21

So, What Is Financially Enough?

EVEN AFTER DOING the exercises outlined throughout this section, you may still struggle with feeling like you don't have enough financially to retire. This is particularly true for those who grew up in poverty or a family with a tight budget. It is hard to navigate deeply set feelings of financial insecurity. How people in your childhood spoke about money and their unspoken reactions to dealing with money and finances created enduring thought patterns.

There are several approaches to dealing with these thought patterns and feelings. One of the most helpful is through what I call comparative gratitude. Look back on where you were in the past and compare that to now. Approach that difference with gratitude. Did you ever live in a studio apartment with just enough money to buy food and clothing? Maybe you didn't live in the best part of town and had to work around the clock to make ends meet.

What did that feel like? Were you miserable and destitute then?

Most likely not. That was just the way things were.

Now, think about your current financial state. Most likely, you live in a much nicer, more spacious home. You can take vacations, spend money when you want, and even give a fair amount to charities you feel close to.

Comparing where you've come from and where you are today with a sense of gratitude turns us away from anxiety and fear. It helps us look ahead with hope.

Suppose you are still feeling unconfident. Another exercise you can do focuses on your resilience. Life events come and go and change your certainty around money. Marriage, children, home ownership, and other major circumstances affect how you spend and save. Try to remember how you successfully navigated through those events. You were able to adapt back then, and you'll be able to adapt today.

What would happen if you had to return to a more financially restrictive lifestyle? Would you feel okay? For most of my clients, the answer is "yes." It wouldn't be fun, but they know they can do it.

Sometimes we'll go as far as to go through their spending plan to make this more real. After listing all the activities and items they want to spend money on in a given ideal year in retirement, they go through the list again and identify which items could be delayed by one year without significant emotional upheaval, and which items are essential. For most people, essential items include keeping their current home, staying healthy, seeing family, and having reasonable food. We put other items on the optional list. We really want to do those things, but if it came down to it, it wouldn't be the end of the world to wait a year or two to do them.

We then add the essential and flexible items and see how much wiggle room the client has. Often, a client's Social Security alone will cover many of these expenses.

By pre-planning optional and flexible areas, you can feel empowered in what you choose to do with your life and your money, even if it isn't what you originally planned. Being grateful for how far you've come and leaning into your resilience can increase confidence and lower worry. You've got this!

CHAPTER 21 REVIEW

- If you still feel unconfident that you have enough financially despite evidence otherwise, think back to when you had less than you do now and reflect on that difference with gratitude.
- Another exercise that can help bridge feelings of financial insufficiency despite evidence otherwise is reflecting on how you navigated major financial life events in the past. You will often find you are more resilient than you give yourself credit for.
- Mentally play out how it would be if you had to be more financially restrictive. Make a list of things you want to

do in an ideal year of retirement and divide it into essential and optional. Review the basic list and compare it to your budget to see how much you have left over. Pre-plan optional and flexible items to empower your life and money choices.

CHAPTER 21 EXERCISES

- Exercise A: Comparative Gratitude
    - Write about a time when you had less. Get into the details about what your life was like. Where did you live? What did you eat? What did you do? Compare this period of life to the present.

- What was your overall experience of life then? How does that compare to your fears for the future?

- Exercise B: Your Financial Resilience
    - How did you respond to significant financial changes in the past? Did you enact a meaningful budgeting tactic? Did you give yourself a specific amount of discretionary income? What investments did you make? Find your good decisions and understand how you asserted control over your finances.

- What lessons did you learn through these significant events? How can you leverage these lessons in the future should you encounter financial hardships?

- Exercise C: The Essential and The Flexible
    - List what you want to do in an ideal year of retirement:

____

____

____

____

____

____

____

____

____

____

____

____

____

    - Divide that list into two separate lists:
        - Essential (e.g., seeing family, food, home, etc.)
        - Optional (e.g., cruise, significant home renovation, etc.)

Essential Optional

____

____

____

- Tally up the essential items and see how much wiggle room your budget has for optional expenditures. How could you adjust if you encountered financial hardship due to a difficult market year or similar?

PART 4

What's Holding You Back?

SOMETIMES IT CAN feel like you have enough, but you still can't commit to retirement. Or, perhaps, you have retired but feel like something is holding you back from the retirement you dreamed of and worked towards.

What is happening? Isn't retirement supposed to be a blissful sailboat ride on fair seas? (All financial and investment companies put that in their marketing brochures!) What is keeping you from living the life you anticipated for decades?

This is all too common. This is what happened to Joyce when she was getting ready to retire.

CHAPTER 22

The Rolling Five-Year-Out Retirement—Feet Dragging in Retirement Planning

MOST PEOPLE REALIZE they have to retire as they get older. Sometimes their jobs are too tough physically, and they can't do it forever. Or, as the saying goes, "I'm too old for this bull [excrement]!" But instead of committing to a date, they talk around it and about it for years. I call it the Rolling Five-Year-Out Retirement.

As I continued to work with Joyce and Jim over the years, this started to happen with Joyce. She kept rolling out her retirement date for five years until she had been talking about it for 10 years cumulatively. It became a huge source of friction between her and Jim because she was not ready to commit to retiring just yet. In one meeting, Jim got agitated and said, "You'll never retire! You keep talking and talking about it, but you're afraid to do it. I want to do things together while we can still travel. We have all of our marbles, and you keep delaying things!"

It's easy to be judgmental and say, "You should just retire and enjoy life," but keeping things in perspective is important. Retirement is a new phenomenon in human history. As lifespans grew and opportunities increased, we made retirement something that we did. It's unfair to say people should retire when they find meaning and a sense of satisfaction from their work.

In light of this, I asked Joyce, "What do you think about what Jim said?"

"Yes, I know I keep talking about retirement, and I want to do things with Jim, but I'm just not there yet. I have a few projects at work I want to wrap up. I still enjoy my work and always wonder whether we'll run out of money. I don't want to be a Walmart greeter!" Joyce replied.

"It sounds like you are still getting fulfillment from work, and working still makes you feel safe," I told her. "I'm wondering a few things. What would make you feel safe financially if you finished the projects at work and things were handed off well to your successor?"

"Well, I feel financially safe and know we have enough. I like the security blanket of having some income. Maybe we could do things together if I cut back on hours a little. Jim and I could do some semi-retirement before jumping into it."

Some people enjoy being on the indefinite work track. They just really like working.

I had a client who did a lot of real estate work. He liked it fine, but didn't like it at the same time. It just felt unnatural not to be busy.

Then, his wife got cancer.

He decided to sell everything so they could travel and do other things. Before that, he wasn't ready to stop being a business owner. When that happened, he realized he was prepared for the transition.

If you want to go until health stops you, that's fine. If your plan is to be taken out on a stretcher, realize you might be alive on that stretcher and plan accordingly. Explore new hobbies, interests, and ways to fill your time. If you're busy with doctors' appointments, medical tests, and procedures, a sudden transition can be okay. But if you're stuck in recovery, it can be like stepping off a cliff. Having nothing to do can lead to depression and anxiety.

You may taper into retirement depending on work demands and other life factors. If you want to spend more time with family, you may not have to retire yet. You could shift your availability at your job, delegate more, or take a different role with more flexibility. Then you could spend more time with your family until you are truly ready to retire.

As Jim struggled with Joyce's feet dragging, I tried my best to reassure him. It's not a transition you can rush people through. For Joyce, work was her chance at self-definition and enabled her to make a big difference in the community. She was reluctant to let go of that.

Jim could be there to support her as her plans change and help give her stepping stones—not just stepping into the void of retirement, but instead having something to do that is important to her, in this case, time together travelling as a couple while still participating in her meaningful work.

As with any transition phase, partners must openly communicate what they need. If Jim had never spoken up, Joyce may not have realized he wanted to spend time with her and may have kept trucking along.

Sometimes, people flounder. We support them as they struggle and flounder. Everyone stalls! Staying stuck in limbo for really long periods can be harmful. Even then, getting people out of a stuck stage can often take a year or two, particularly if they're scared.

A large event jars people out of it, and sometimes, not. There is no single magic question that leads to an epiphany when it comes to retirement slow-stepping. If your loved one is delaying, the essential thing is to be consistently supportive and know when to confront the disconnects you see.

CHAPTER 22 REVIEW

- Retirement isn't something to be forced on yourself or others. You can choose to work until you can't anymore, but make contingency plans in case you're suddenly forced into retirement to safeguard your emotional, mental, and physical health.
- Full retirement isn't your only option if that isn't what you want. If you want more free time but still want to work, explore midway options like scaling back or transitioning to a new role.
- If someone you love is delaying, work on communicating your concerns and feelings while listening to their thoughts, experiences, and opinions.

CHAPTER 22 DISCUSSION QUESTIONS

1. Are you slow-stepping retirement? If so, is it keeping you from living the life you envisioned?

2. Do you have a plan and things to do if you are forced to retire before you are fully ready due to health or other life events?

CHAPTER 23

Escape Flailing and Floundering—Find Balance for an Intentional Transition

LIKE MANY PEOPLE who slow-step retirement, I have also seen people who retire but do not know what to do with themselves. When this happens, I generally see people fall into two categories: Flounderers or Flailers.

Flounderers are people who do too little. They step into retirement and feel enclosed and claustrophobic. Sometimes they lose motivation because they don't have work to drive them. Some turn to drinking. Others don't exercise, watch too much TV, and rapidly gain weight. This can turn to more serious mental health struggles like depression, which I discuss later in the chapter.

On the opposite side of the spectrum, there are Flailers. These people will become overstimulated like a dog barking and chasing its tail. "Oh my god, I got a new house renovation, and then we're going to do this and that project," they tell me. They ping-pong between too many things because they don't know where to divert the time and energy that used to go toward work. Flailers will constantly have new projects they are starting, whether or not the previous projects are finished.

Other Flailers have fallen prey to the general anxiety of not bringing in income. They find the prospect of not having an income overwhelming. Even when they know their financial situation and we review their investments to show them that they can now passively make enough to pay their bills, it doesn't alleviate their worries about not having enough. This fear-based intensity is powerful.

Sometimes, this fear guides people to start new businesses when they retire or buy rental properties. They are constantly scanning the horizon for the next thing. Suddenly, they are just as busy and unhappy as they were before retirement.

When one of my clients is flailing this way, I ask them a few simple questions. "What if you just took a break and didn't do a project for three months?" I'll ask. If the person's eyes widen, we have a serious flailing situation.

Then, there is a third type of flailing: portfolio flailing. People stuck in portfolio flailing are always reading investment news and watching their accounts. While this sounds fine on the outside, it can be detrimental to people mentally and financially because too much news media tends to breed fear. Most financial news online is notorious for not being just pure news but intentionally crafted messages to grab your attention, so the articles generate more advertising revenue. This is unhealthy when viewed from an over-wellness perspective and can lead to poor financial decisions.

For example, some portfolio Flailers get sucked into investing heavily in gold. People can see many ads for gold. Before they recognize it, they feel like they have to buy gold. It scratches an itch, and "Oh my god, I have to be safe with my money!" The portfolio Flailers later tell me. However, suppose they were to study gold's performance a bit further. In that case, gold's volatility is similar or higher than that of stocks and, over time, sometimes underperforms that of stocks for decades. It can also struggle to beat inflation consistently.

Later, portfolio Flailers come into my office with what can only be described as Frankenstein finances. They've chopped stuff up, thrown it together, and suddenly it's alive, walking, and burning down the local villages! After reviewing their portfolios, I saw someone who was bad at building furniture and mixing parts for four different Ikea pieces after throwing out the instructions. If they're lucky, they have a wobbly bed attached to a nightstand with a built-in lamp. None of it seems to work.

If you manage your finances yourself, seeing a financial professional to help check your work can be helpful. This is particularly true when you have to make big decisions under time pressure. Some financial planners are happy to check the math for you, give you the computer printout, and let you know you're on the right path. I take a co-pilot approach, which involves diving into assumptions and the total life picture.

Can you procrastinate if you don't need to make an immediate decision? This can stop your Portfolio Flailing from being implemented too quickly and getting stuck. Instead of deflecting to the binary and trapped feeling, consider whether it is the only option or if there is something else you could do that would give you greater flexibility.

Flexibility is particularly key if you are suddenly thrown into retirement. You won't have time to process everything and know exactly what you want. Go for flexibility even if they are not the ideal options. You want a reasonable and prudent option that can allow you to live to fight another day. If you plan on leveraging healthy procrastination, put a backstop and get it on your calendar. Otherwise, it's easy to procrastinate forever.

Whether Flounderers or Flailers, when people are faced with uncertainty they turn to what has worked for them. Whatever tools you bring into retirement are the ones you will use, unless you take this as an opportunity to learn new tools and/or tweak how you use your tools. For example, if being busy has served you well in the past, that is likely what you will do in retirement. If having a strong drink has helped you relax, it can be easy to turn to that with the anxiety from the newfound free time.

We offer a trial period of retirement for people who are worried they will fall into one of these categories. What would happen if you tried not working for three months? How much can you slow down and delegate at work?

When I see clients floundering or flailing in retirement, I try to reel them back in. How did they envision their retirement going? How can they leverage strategies that made them successful in the past to get back on track? Exploring these questions and applying them to the correct situations is really impactful in getting clients over the hump of retirement floundering or flailing.

In these situations, we may need someone we trust to act as a lifeguard and tell us, "Stop floundering and flailing. Let me put on the floaty thing and kick back to the shore."

Our brains will do all sorts of mental gymnastics to close that gap. It is a cognitive dissonance that's tough to escape for things they are not aware of about themselves. It's your autopilot, and you may not realize what you're doing. It's like finding a toddler drawing with a crayon on the wall. You can ask them why they did it, and they will come up with various excuses, but they probably only did it because it felt like a good idea at the time.

If you slip on ice, sometimes you need to regain your balance instead of trying to run like a Looney Tunes character until you face plant. Slow down, sprinkle some salt, and catch your breath to skate off the ice to solid ground.

CHAPTER 23 REVIEW

- I commonly see two types of stuck people: Flounderers and Flailers. Flounderers are people who don't do enough. They get overwhelmed and stop trying to do anything in retirement. Flailers try to do too much, which can manifest as too many projects, obsessing over income, and portfolio flailing.
- When we are stuck in these situations, it helps to have someone to help us get back on track and escape cognitive distortions.

CHAPTER 23 DISCUSSION QUESTIONS

1. If you find yourself floundering and flailing in the new, murky retirement water, go back to what you initially wanted to do. Is what you are doing right now in alignment with that vision?

ESCAPE FLAILING AND FLOUNDERING

CHAPTER 24

Getting Unstuck—You've Navigated Change Before

YOU ARE IN the middle of a major life transition, which will lead to changes. But this isn't the first significant change you've been through! The trick is to identify success points and use those tools.

When you are stuck, one way to move past these hangups is to ask yourself: How do you deal with change? Consider when you dealt with significant modifications and identify how you navigated successfully during those periods. Explore what strengths or strategies you drew on during these times. Think also about the particularly challenging changes. What made them difficult?

If obstacles stopped you, then what tools do you need to change? Do you need a therapist to help you sift through things?

Do you need a coach to help you get physically fit to join the local bike club?

By examining both successes and struggles, you gain valuable self-insight. You bring unique resilience and adaptability. This reflection can help you recognize response patterns and better address the current challenges in your life. It can empower you to make better and more confident decisions.

CHAPTER 24 REVIEW

- If you get stuck, it can help to reflect on what you've done that has helped in the past. Consider the obstacles, what you did to navigate them, and the outcome of those experiences.

CHAPTER 24 DISCUSSION QUESTIONS

- How have you navigated change before at your best? How have you handled change at your worst? What did you learn from those experiences?

- How do those past experiences compare to your situation today? How can you integrate the lessons you learned into your present situation?

CHAPTER 25

Overcoming Obstacles—A Step-by-Step Approach

SOMETIMES, IT CAN feel like an exhausting number of obstacles are keeping you from living the life you want, beyond getting unstuck. When you are trying to move on but feel overwhelmed, one thing that can help is identifying and organizing the obstacles ahead of you.

If things are holding you back from your ideal retirement, write them out, preferably somewhere with a lot of space, like a whiteboard. Permit yourself to list the obstacles, whether they are big or just feel big. For example, in your ideal retirement, you would own a second home in your favorite vacation destination. However, you aren't sure how much it would cost and how you would manage it while you weren't there.

Once you have a list of things holding you back, start brainstorming how to address them. A client wanted to move close to her grandkids but kept feeling overwhelmed. She didn't know how to redo her trust and estate plan, which she needed to do since her husband passed away, and people had moved. She also needed to figure out the logistics of her move, but was overwhelmed by the volume of things to do. She couldn't make a decision and was stuck in a loop.

We reviewed the things keeping her from her goal of living near her grandkids and listed them on a whiteboard in my office. The first thing on her list of roadblocks was that she wasn't sure how much it would cost to buy a house where they lived. We went to Zillow and called a realtor. Between the two sources, we roughly estimated how much it would take to live near her grandkids.

Using this figure, we identified how much we needed to set aside when she sold her house and how we would restructure her finances accordingly. This was also an opportune moment to discuss how her trust was set up and what steps she needed to take to address it.

When you're faced with an overwhelming situation with innumerable things to deal with, the best way to face it is to break it down into small pieces. To return to the vacation house example, consider what time of year you want to visit this new home and how soon you wish to own it. Use these two rough dates to start planning when you will buy the house. Do you know any realtors in that area or know someone who does? Do you need someone to sit with you as you call them? Look up management companies that could look after your vacation home while you aren't there, and start getting quotes from them.

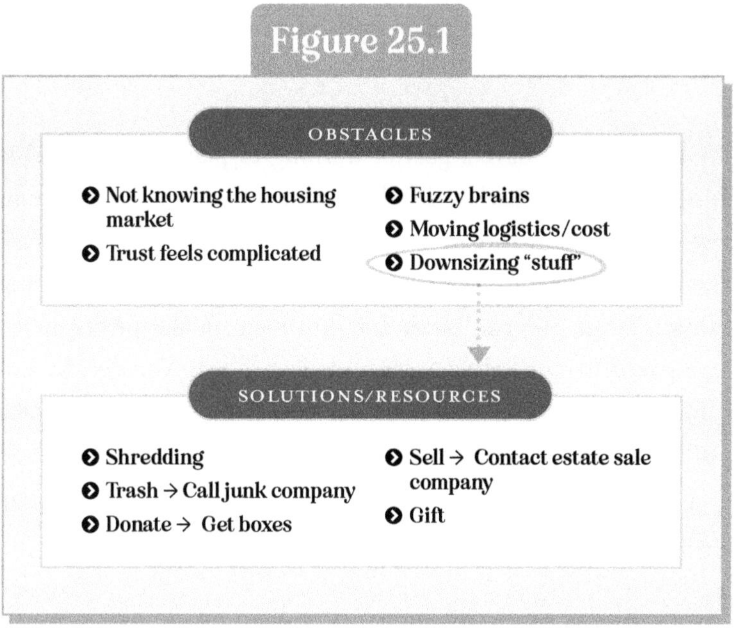

As I show above, it can also help to work through the problem using a whiteboard, as I show with this example on deciding whether or not you want to move. For obstacles, I wrote: (1) not knowing the real estate market where I want to move to, (2) having a complicated trust that makes me feel like I can't use money to buy a house, (3) my brain feels fuzzy, (4) confusion about moving logistics and the cost, (5) downsizing is overwhelming.

With those top-level issues and concerns written out, I brainstorm on the bottom half how we could address them. We could address the downsizing fears by working through manageable steps like (1) shredding documents that need to be shredded, (2) calling a junk removal company, (3) donating unwanted things, (4) selling stuff through a living estate sale, or (5) gifting things that you would eventually give to heirs anyway that you don't use or enjoy.

If one process component still seems insurmountable, break it into smaller pieces or find a new approach to make it doable.

Let's say you have a goal of learning to play the guitar. One thing holding you back is deciding what sort of guitar you should buy. You brainstormed your plan to figure it out and decided the best thing to do is to visit a local music shop, but you can't bring yourself to go. You can break this into even smaller pieces by listening to different styles of guitar playing to help you decide, and talking to a friend of yours who is a musician. Or you could take a different approach and ask a friend to go with you to the music shop to look at the other guitars. Sometimes, having company makes all the difference.

Addressing and exploring the obstacles can lead to greater self-insight. If you find the idea of moving insurmountable, perhaps you are not ready to move yet because of what it signifies to you internally, such as a change in life or what your current home means. Pay attention to that self-insight without letting it hold you back from living the life of your dreams.

CHAPTER 25 REVIEW

- If you still feel truly mired, list things you think are making you stuck and brainstorm how to address them. If anything seems too big, try breaking it into smaller pieces until it is manageable. Highlight or circle topics that require further research or outside help.

- Use this as an opportunity for self-discovery. What areas seem to hold you back?

CHAPTER 25 DISCUSSION QUESTIONS

1. Are there any obstacles holding you back from your ideal retirement? If so, how can you navigate around and through these obstacles?

CHAPTER 26

Recognizing Retirement Blues—The Hidden Threat of Depression

SOME PEOPLE FACE an even more difficult problem. Despite the best planning and preparation, the reality of retirement can be a shocking and jarring transition. The shift from a structured work life to an unstructured day creates a profound sense of loss and disorientation. Many people can feel disconnected, purposeless, isolated, and lonely—which, for some, can lead to depression.

Depression is characterized by sadness, low energy, or lack of interest that lasts for weeks and isn't situationally dependent. While some might describe retirement as a situation, it is more than that. It is a new phase of life. This is distinctly different from experiencing something tragic, such as the death of a pet. If that happens, you will likely be very sad for a while as you grieve. That is okay. It is a natural reaction. Depression is different from grief, which eases over time. Depression feels unshakeable.[6]

A common sign of depression is losing interest in activities you used to do consistently. For example, a person who used to like running suddenly doesn't want to run at all. Or, they used to play chess daily and now can't be bothered. These sudden drops in interest might indicate depression. A consistent loss of interest in previously enjoyable things, when everything in life becomes tasteless, is sometimes called anhedonia and can indicate depression.

Depression should not be conflated with feelings of frustration that come from trying something new. If you are learning woodworking, it can make you frustrated and profoundly discouraged as you make mistakes while you try to learn a complex new skill. Learning to do new things can be frustrating, and it is easy to lose motivation. However, this differs from suddenly losing interest in long-loved hobbies and things.

A sign of depression is when you're physically well, but you feel awful all the time. You might experience constant aches and pains that constantly bother you. You gain or lose weight significantly, feel fatigued, struggle with excessive guilt, or have a tough time concentrating. These feelings and sensations can be debilitating. Sometimes depression can even lead to thoughts about death beyond the fear of dying.

6 Elizabeth A. O'Connor et al., "Screening for Depression in Adults and Older Adults in Primary Care: An Updated Systematic Review," *Evidence Synthesis* 75 (2009): https://www.ncbi.nlm.nih.gov/books/NBK36406/table/ch1.t1.

Another sign of depression is sleeping too much or too little. This can be a tricky symptom to track for several reasons. Sleep patterns can naturally change as you age because of changing circadian rhythms, leading to evolving sleep quality and duration. Older adults may have difficulty falling asleep, wake more often at night, or rise earlier in the morning, which can cause exhaustion unrelated to depression.

Transition stress can also lead to sleep changes. Retirement can trigger a lot of anxiety and lead to difficulty sleeping. Once I was laid off during a force reduction, and I started my own business. To say the least, I was very stressed out. When that happened, I had what was called a sleep inversion. I started sleeping during the day and staying up all night. I would go to bed at 3 a.m. and sleep until 10 a.m. While this is similar to depression, it was not the same.

If you or someone you love is struggling with depression, you must consult with or encourage that person to see a licensed professional. Professional help can be the best way to address a serious mental health condition like depression through therapy, medication, or a combination of both. It provides invaluable support and guidance. Therapy can also help develop coping strategies and provide a space for listening. Remember that reaching out for help is a sign of strength and an essential step toward creating well-being.

Beyond therapy, there are some additional steps you can take that can help alleviate symptoms of depression. However, using these strategies in concert with medical advice is essential. First, ensure you get at least 20 minutes of sunlight daily. This can boost serotonin and improve your mood. Second, eating well without too much sugar and emphasizing whole foods can also impact positively. Third, monitoring caffeine intake can go a long way, as excessive caffeine can lead to anxiety and lost sleep. Fourth, exercise can release endorphins and reduce fatigue. Even simple activities like going for a walk can be practical. Finally, social interaction is also essential. Friends, family, and other supportive people provide emotional support and reduce isolation. I use the "five S" acronym to remember these items: sun, sustenance (food), sleep, sweat (exercise), and social interaction.

If you are feeling low, make a checklist of those things. See whether any are missing and aim to incorporate them into your life every day. For example, if you don't drink much plain water but instead drink six cups of coffee daily, reducing caffeine might be the first place to start. For myself and many of my clients, sleep is an essential component of mental well-being. These can form a baseline for better wellness, giving more space to existential questions.

CHAPTER 26 REVIEW

- The transition to retirement can also trigger depression in some people. Depression is a lasting emotional state that isn't situation-dependent, commonly associated with (1) a sudden lack of interest in things that once brought joy, (2) bodily discomfort, and/or (3) changes in sleep patterns.
- Depression is a serious condition, and therapy is often the best option. Beyond therapy, some things that may help include (1) getting 20 minutes of sunlight daily, (2)

eating and drinking healthily, (3) monitoring caffeine intake, (4) exercising, and (5) spending time with friends and family.

CHAPTER 26 DISCUSSION QUESTIONS

1. If you have retired, what has your mood been like since retirement?

2. Make a daily checklist to get these essential things and do them for two weeks. How do you feel after the two weeks compared to before?
   - 20 minutes of sunlight
   - Eat healthy meals
   - Limit caffeine intake and get regular sleep
   - Exercise
   - Socialize

PART 5

Navigating Financial Anxieties

My clients, Martha and Timothy, scheduled a last-minute meeting with me on Tuesday. As I took their raincoats and led them to their seats, I could tell they were tense.

Martha had retired several years before, and Timothy was approaching his retirement date in two years. Timothy led the conversation immediately. "I just don't feel ready for retirement," he started. "What if there is a serious emergency and we haven't saved enough money? How do people go on vacations without income coming in?"

As he continued to express his money fears and hangups, his shoulders crept closer and closer to his ears, and he hunched forward with his arms crossed. His breath came faster as he described each possible doomsday scenario until I finally cut in.

Financial fears can creep in even as you prepare to take the plunge into retirement. Despite what financial advisors and your accounts tell you, you may obsess over whether you are financially prepared.

Rather than patronizingly telling clients, "You have enough money, you'll be fine!", I've found a different approach helpful. I assist clients in shifting to a curious, exploratory posture. With the right frame of mind, the future can change from danger and uncertainty to opportunity and meaning. (That's why financial planning is an ongoing process and not just a document that gets updated once a year. It is a method for exploring what will be meaningful as life throws changes our way!)

Like many people embarking on or on the precipice of retirement, you may be anxious about money. This part of the workbook will discuss common retirement money fears and how to tackle them.

CHAPTER 27

Money Fears and Freedom—How Your Past Influences Your Retirement Future

CLIENTS FREQUENTLY COME to me with their retirement fears, which are usually centered around their financial well-being. The transition from a steady income to living off savings can be overwhelming and create feelings of fear and anxiety. Many soon-to-be and recent retirees are concerned their finances won't sustain them through the years and all of the life events that could happen.

Financial fears and anxieties can make many feel vulnerable as they navigate the next chapter of their lives. What interests me is that some people have a visceral fear of money, while others do not.

Our experiences are one source of this tightly held fear. Our childhoods give us a financial framework that can shape how we think about money for the rest of our lives. This fear can stem from many experiences and contexts surrounding money.

For example, how did your parents talk about and treat money? This is particularly salient if there were emotional responses related to money, such as arguments or unhealthy relationship dynamics. Was money a harsh gatekeeper that dictated what you could or couldn't do? Was it a source of security, a means to gain parental approval, or something else?

Your early money memories and how money was managed around you can reveal insights into your relationship with money. There are subliminal messages when people say, "We can't buy that until we have a certain amount of money in our bank account," "We can't go on vacation until we've paid off the mortgage," or "Payday is next Tuesday, and the mortgage payment goes out Wednesday so we can eat steak today."

This was the situation for Timothy. When I asked him what he remembered about money growing up, he said money was infrequently present and often fleeting during his childhood. Timothy recalled his parents' long, explosive arguments as they struggled to make ends meet. He looked introspective as he remembered, "It was like clockwork. My parents started yelling and slamming doors the day or two before payday. It got worse around the holidays. I felt guilty at Christmas getting presents when I knew it caused my parents to fight."

Money was at stake, and it was emotional for Timothy. He wanted to control every penny so they wouldn't struggle like his parents had.

Conversely, some people don't talk about money, particularly around their children. This can stem from avoidance because they feel shame, discomfort, or stress around money. This was the situation for Martha. Martha's parents always told her and her siblings that money talk was uncouth. While Timothy talked about his anxieties, she shifted uncomfortably in her seat. Some clients are more comfortable discussing what goes on in their bedroom than their bank account!

Building awareness of how we think about money can help us see what runs in the background of our thoughts on autopilot. We call these money scripts, and they explain some of our automatic reactions to money. These are usually programmed at a young age. It's not a bug—it's a feature of your system that helps you understand emotional or visceral reactions to money.

For example, a client repeatedly discussed a $600 dresser with me. She loved this dresser. The size, wood, and style were all perfect. She went to the showroom frequently to check whether it was still there, but anxiety told her that the dresser was unnecessary and expensive.

But her investment statements said she had enough money to buy six or seven *thousand* dressers.

I discussed it with her at length after she had continued to mention it for months without buying it. I asked her why she hadn't bought it yet, to which she replied that it wasn't necessary.

"Is money only for necessary things?" I asked. "You're willing to help your kids furnish their houses and go on vacations."

"Well, that's different," she replied, but she seemed to take in what I was saying.

I decided to press her a bit further. "Compared to your net worth, would spending $600 make a difference, and what do you feel that difference will be?" I asked. She hesitated as she considered the question.

She finally bought it a few weeks later.

Money scripts can come from our religious backgrounds. In my past religious experience, wealth was viewed in one of four ways:

1. A sign of divine favor. If you weren't wealthy, it was because you were sinning or not giving enough away, and therefore, you were subject to punishment.
2. A dangerous state that will probably lead you astray from finding purpose and meaning in life and will destroy you.
3. Something you should give away.
4. A sign of your character—anyone who isn't good with money is wasting the blessings bestowed upon them.

I would encourage those with spiritual backgrounds to explore what messages their experiences told them and remember their state of being when they were first taught those messages. Were they children, so they didn't understand the wisdom behind what was being taught? Was there only one aspect being taught? Perhaps it is time to take a more comprehensive look at wealth and money from your faith community and recalibrate what you believe about money and wealth.

During this self-evaluation, it is also helpful to remember what helped to make you successful in the first place. You have worked hard and saved carefully to reach this point. What was that journey like? What traits did you rely on? Consider also how you would handle money differently if you were to do it all over again. You may have encouraged yourself to do right by guarding and growing your money. If that is true, you might see money as more of a duty instead of what money is—a thing that supports what you want to do with yourself.

CHAPTER 27 REVIEW

- Shame and anxiety around money can stem from childhood and other informative experiences. These become scripts that inform how we think about and discuss (or don't discuss) money.
- Money scripts are the autopilot thoughts when we think about money. If you become aware of these scripts, you can start to take control of how they shape your life.
- Religious upbringing can have a significant impact on your life as well. Explore what financial messages were shared or perceived in your childhood religious experience and how those inform you today.

CHAPTER 27 DISCUSSION QUESTIONS[7]

1. What did your childhood teach you about money? Follow the example below to chart out your childhood experiences of money. For this exercise, you will do the following:
   a. Divide your life into periods: Separate your life into developmental periods, e.g., infancy and childhood (0 to 6 years), late childhood (7 to 11 years), adolescence (12 to 17 years), early adulthood (18 to 24; 25 to 30 years), and so on, continuing in decades. Feel free to use our template on the following pages or create your own and adjust periods as needed.
   b. Identify and map out financial memories: Write down any money-related memories that still carry emotional weight (like financial flashpoints) for each period. These memories could be specific events or general feelings you had about money during that time. Place these memories on the page based on whether they were positive, neutral, or negative (see example on next page). Include what you felt during the event and how you feel about it now. Don't dismiss memories that might seem insignificant. Write them down if you feel something when you think about them now.
   c. Use prompts if needed. If you're struggling to recall memories, ask yourself: What's the most recent financial event that caused me stress? When did I feel this same feeling before? When did I first remember feeling fear, shame, sadness, pride, joy, or hope around money?

7 The Financial Therapy Clinical Institute and Nathan Astle, Certified Financial Therapist. Used by permission

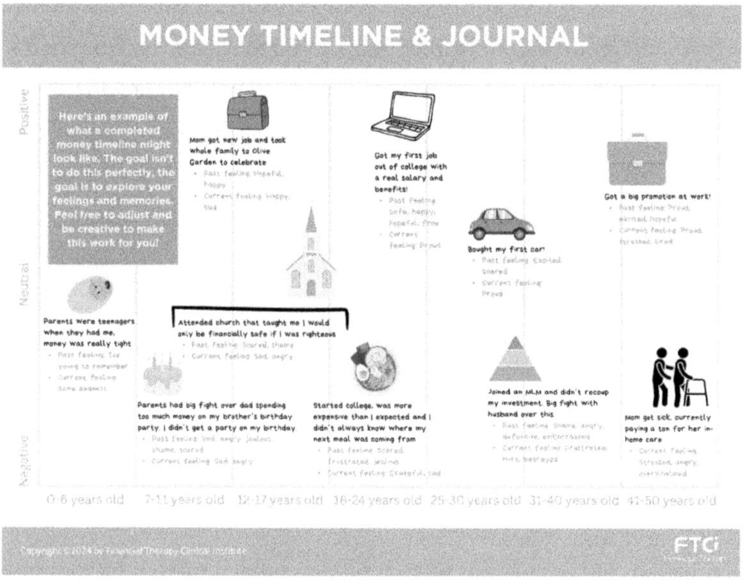
MONEY TIMELINE & JOURNAL
Positive
Neutral
Negative
Here's an example of what a completed money timeline might look like. The goal isn't to do this perfectly, the goal is to explore your feelings and memories. Feel free to adjust and be creative to make this work for you!
Mom got new job and took whole family to Olive Garden to celebrate
Past feeling: Hopeful, happy
Current feeling: Happy, sad
Got my first job out of college with a real salary and benefits!
Past feeling: Safe, happy, hopeful, free
Current feeling: Proud
Got a big promotion at work!
Past feeling: Proud, excited, hopeful
Current feeling: Proud, stressed, tired
Bought my first car!
Past feeling: Excited, scared
Current feeling: Proud
Parents were teenagers when they had me, money was really tight
Past feeling: Too young to remember
Current feeling: Some sadness
Attended church that taught me I would only be financially safe if I was righteous
Past feeling: Scared, shame
Current feeling: Sad, angry
Parents had big fight over dad spending too much money on my brother's birthday party. I didn't get a party on my birthday.
Past feeling: Sad, angry, jealous, shame, scared
Current feeling: Sad, angry
Started college, was more expensive than I expected and I didn't always know where my next meal was coming from
Past feeling: Scared, frustrated, jealous
Current feeling: Grateful, sad
Joined an MLM and didn't recoup my investment. Big fight with husband over this
Past feeling: Shame, angry, defensive, embarrassed
Current feeling: Frustrated, hurt, betrayed
Mom got sick, currently paying a ton for her in-home care
Current feeling: Stressed, angry, overwhelmed
0-6 years old
7-11 years old
12-17 years old
18-24 years old
25-30 years old
31-40 years old
41-50 years old
Copyright © 2024 by Financial Therapy Clinical Institute
FTCI

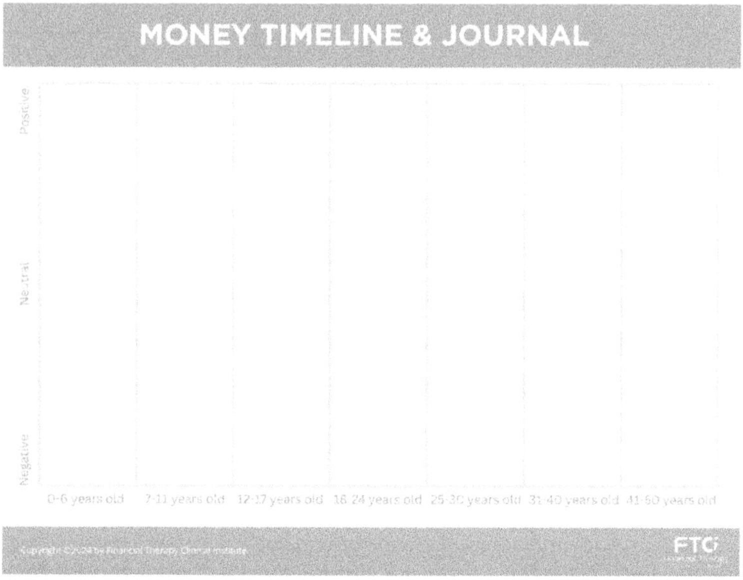
MONEY TIMELINE & JOURNAL
Positive
Neutral
Negative
0-6 years old
7-11 years old
12-17 years old
18-24 years old
25-30 years old
31-40 years old
41-50 years old
Copyright © 2024 by Financial Therapy Clinical Institute
FTCI

2. Once you've completed your timeline, review it to identify recurring emotions. Are there emotions, such as shame or fear, that you see consistently throughout your timeline? Reflect on the beliefs that may have developed due to these memories. Can you identify any current beliefs about money or yourself connected to these memories?

3. Consider how your past emotions and beliefs influence your current relationship with money. Do the same emotions or beliefs arise in your present-day financial behaviors? Are any financial behaviors in your present driven by these emotions or beliefs?

4. When you think about your future timeline, what changes would you like to see in these emotions and beliefs? What actions could you take to start shifting these patterns (e.g., see a financial therapist, keep a money journal, use mindfulness when shopping)?

5. Do you consider any or all of your wealth as more than just money? If so, what is it, and how does that manifest in your life?

CHAPTER 28

The Hidden Barriers to Financial Peace—Recognizing the Cognitive Distortions Holding You Back

FEAR CAN HOLD us back from living our best and most fulfilling lives. Many people struggle in particular with fear surrounding money. Money is important. It dictates many aspects of how we can live our lives. This is an area of intense emotion and anxiety for many.

The fear surrounding money and its careful management often leads to cognitive distortions or negative biases in financial management. Cognitive distortions are adverse, knee-jerk emotional and behavioral reactions that can be troublesome for anyone. They can take many forms and affect finances in many ways.

However, you can diminish money fear and anxiety with the right tools, strategies, and outlook.

There are many cognitive distortions, but here are a few of the most common ones I see day-to-day:

- Scarcity mindset: The idea that money is limited and not proportionate to actual wealth. This is characterized by an inability to spend money and enjoy life to its fullest potential (e.g., "I can't turn on lights at night because it costs too much" when the individual has millions in savings).
- Fortune telling: When a person predicts an outcome without considering or researching its actual likelihood, this is often an emotion-based prediction. For example, a neighbor says, "You have to invest right now in gold because of the upcoming election."
- Extremism or jumping to conclusions: When a person makes assumptions about the effects of an event or someone's opinions. For example, someone says, "My husband always wastes money," or "The stock market dipped for a few days. It is going to tank forever!"
- Focus on the negative: When a person focuses solely on the negative side of any situation, such as the washing machine breaking or the house flooding, and they must spend part of their emergency fund.
- Should-ing: When a person continually thinks about what they "should" do without taking action (e.g., I should get more exercise; I should eat better; I should build a sensible budget).

- Entry/Exit paralysis: The feeling that one can't or shouldn't change anything. For example, someone sets up a portfolio and then feels as though they can't buy or sell anything ever again.

These cognitive distortions shape the way people approach their finances, often to detrimental effect.

So, how do we approach cognitive distortions? There are three approaches that I take:

First, if I hear these cognitive distortions from clients for the first time, I ask clarifying questions. This can help me fully engage with the thought and bring it to its full conclusion.

For example, someone might jump to conclusions and think it will be a disaster if a certain political party wins the next election. "What does a disaster look like?" I might ask. They explain that the stock market will crash and they will lose their hard-earned money. "When the stock market crashes," I continue, "what happens? How much would you lose? If it did recover, how long would it take? And if that happened, what would you do next?"

By providing an outlet and helping them to reason it out themselves, I can usually help them recognize that the stock market might dip or crash, but it probably won't be forever. For many, a stock market crash wouldn't impact their spending in the short term. For others, it may mean they must delay a vacation or a home renovation project for a year or two until things calm down in the market and start recovering. Or if a client buys a dresser and does not like it, I ask them about the return policies or the impact of a negative furniture experience.

Second, we sometimes have to choose not to engage with thoughts. Mindfulness is all the rage nowadays, but this is an area where it can transition from faddish to useful! Being able to identify a cognitive distortion and then choose not to engage with it can be a decisive step toward reducing financial anxiety. If one practices mindfulness, one can apply the skill to financial thoughts.

Managing our thoughts can be similar to riding on a train. You aren't supposed to get on every train that pulls into the train station. Instead, you should look for the train to take you to where you want to go. You observe that a train is incorrect, so you let it stop at the station and pull away. Don't get on every financial train that pulls into the station of your mind.

The goal of observing your money behaviors is to consider them from another perspective. Are your money behaviors truly aligned with what you want to do with your money? What does money mean to you? If you were to teach yourself about money as a child or young adult, what would you say now that you have life experience?

Third, carefully curate the news and social media that you consume. Nothing gets your attention like bad news and warnings of the imminent end of civilization. 24-hour news, financial news, short videos, and social media posts capitalize on this. Algorithms feed us stories and posts that think will keep our attention, so the company gets more ad revenue. We must proactively curate what news we watch, when, and what we allow on social media.

I personally carefully curate my social media not to include political or financial news since it is algorithm-driven and self-reinforcing. Instead, I purposefully go to particular news and financial sites and services that are less attention-seeking and more informative.

Related to this, it also helps to be cautious of two other tendencies: index tracking and market watching.

When people know I'm a financial advisor, they often greet me with, "Wow, did you see what the Dow did today?"

While this is an odd greeting and I usually prefer, "Hi, Chris, how are you today?", I appreciate that people feel more informed when they are index tracking, which is when they get daily updates on major market indices.

Be cautious if you are index tracking, and don't overreact when the indexes have dramatic swings, or let them dictate your emotional outcome. Many forget that one day in the market is not as significant as the cumulative return of the market. But if you ask them what the same index did year-to-date or over the last 10 years, they would have no idea. The smaller perspective feels better but has little to no bearing on what you should do with your investments or how your investment even performed that same day.

Another tendency that I see more often than index tracking is market watching. Market watching involves closely observing the market and monitoring your portfolio, which can lead to negative physiological consequences. It helps to take frequent breaks from financial news, as it is often written to attract viewership rather than tell the holistic, honest financial picture.

Investing is often like farming—you plant something and let it grow for a long time. The financial news constantly asks us to restructure our investments, telling us that things won't bode well for us if we don't. Realistically, changing your investments too often is one of the best indicators that you will underperform. Constantly watching your account makes you feel like you should be doing something with it.

CHAPTER 28 REVIEW

- Cognitive distortions are mental versions of knee-jerk reactions that can keep us from making the best decisions. Common cognitive distortions include:
    - Scarcity mindset: The idea that money is limited and not proportionate to actual wealth.
    - Fortune telling: When a person emotionally predicts an outcome without considering/researching its actual likelihood.
    - Extremism/Jumping to conclusions: When a person makes assumptions about an event's effect or someone's opinions.
    - Focus on the negative: When a person focuses solely on the negative side of any situation.

- Should-ing: When a person keeps thinking about what they "should" do without taking action.
- Entry/Exit paralysis: The feeling that one can't/shouldn't change anything.

- There are three approaches to dealing with cognitive distortions:
  - Ask clarifying questions to get to the root of your reasoning.
  - Choose not to engage with thoughts by leveraging mindfulness.
  - Carefully curate your information intake.
- In addition to these approaches, be cautious of two other habits that can increase financial anxiety and decrease decision-making:
  - Index tracking: Closely following the performance of stock indices throughout short periods.
  - Market watching: Closely following a particular stock or portfolio performance over short periods.

CHAPTER 28 DISCUSSION QUESTIONS

1. Are any cognitive distortions holding you back and/or those you love? If so, what does that look like?

____

____

____

____

____

2. How do your upbringing and past influence how you think about money?

3. Is there anyone in your life whom you see falling into a cognitive distortion? What does that look like?

4. Brainstorm ideas to address cognitive distortions in your life below:

CHAPTER 29

Avoiding the Chaos—Organizing Your Life Before Retirement

ONE OF THE best ways to circumvent financial anxiety in retirement is to be well-organized beforehand. You should begin serious planning three to five years before retirement starts. This gives you the time to do things gradually and practice some of what you want in retirement while you still have the backstop of income from work.

Part 3 discussed two primary tools to help people get organized: a net worth statement (list what you own versus what you owe) and a cash flow diagram, showing income sources and the spending required to live your life.

I've included 5- and 10-year retirement preparation checklists in the appendix to this book. With a longer retirement on-ramp, you can transition your investments into more conservative and stable accounts and do other important legal or financial tasks, like preparing wills. If you can provide plenty of time to tackle these goals, you will be able to consider how you want to position your assets.

Along similar lines, many clients ask me, "What paperwork do I need to keep and what can I get rid of? I can't keep track of everything with all the papers everywhere!" I try to break things down into what is essential to keep and what is no longer relevant. Here are some guidelines:

1. Always keep wills, trusts, divorce decrees, and other legal documents.
2. Keep payoff letters from loans, particularly mortgages and student loans.
3. Keep supporting documents for the prior three years of tax returns if you have a straightforward tax situation or the last seven years if you have a more complex one. This would include 1099s, K-1s, W-2s, and business accounting files (such as business checking account statements, profit and loss statements, and balance sheets).
4. Keep recent bank and investment statements (within the last year). Throw away the oldest one every time you get a new one.
5. Old investment statements can be shredded as long as you have a cost basis for the investment. Consult your tax professional and financial advisor to verify.
6. Scan old statements on a high-speed scanner, back-up copies securely to the cloud, then shred everything!

To stay organized for taxes, get a highly recognizable folder because of its bright color, a funny picture on the front, or its material. Put any documents into it as they come in (receipts for tax-deductible medical expenses, donation receipts, 1099s, etc.) and keep the folder near where you handle your mail when you bring it in the house. This way, all paper documents are in one place, and you can give them directly to your tax preparer. I do the same for electronic tax documents—as soon as they arrive, I drop them into one electronic folder labelled prominently with the year.

CHAPTER 29 REVIEW

- If you have yet to retire, planning is the best way to prevent retirement financial anxiety. In the appendix, I've included 5- and 10-year-out retirement plans to assist with planning.
- As you prepare, this can be a helpful time to pare down to only what you need. Some things that should be saved include:
    - Wills, trusts, divorce decrees, and other legal documents.
    - Payoff letters from loans, particularly mortgages and student loans.
- If you have a simple tax situation, supporting documents for the prior three years of tax returns, or the last seven years if it's more complex. This includes 1099s, K-1s, W-2s, and business accounting files (such as business checking account statements, profit and loss statements, and balance sheets).

- Recent bank and investment statements (within the last year).
- Old investment statements can be shredded as long as you have a cost basis for the investment. Talk to your tax professional and financial advisor to check.
- Scan old statements on a high-speed scanner, back-up copies securely to the cloud, and then shred everything!

CHAPTER 29 DISCUSSION QUESTIONS

1. If you plan for retirement, how far along are you? Refer to the checklists in the appendix. What are some things that need to be done to prepare for retirement?

CHAPTER 30

Going Past Financial Lockdown—Get Used to Spending Money While Not Working

JIM, WHO HAD initially thrived in retirement, soon returned to my office with Joyce. He was panicked by the sudden transition from steady paychecks to relying on savings and pensions, and made the drastic decision to stop spending money altogether. He was overwhelmed by the idea that he had to conserve every dollar to avoid running out of funds.

These thoughts and feelings cause people to drastically lower their quality of life as they reduce essential expenses, limit activities, and avoid the things that would otherwise bring them joy. This leads to a cycle of fear, preventing them from enjoying life.

For retirees facing financial anxiety, I transfer a fixed amount of money to their checking accounts each month for them to spend as they see fit. At first, many clients hesitate or feel anxious about the new arrangement. They struggle to make the mental shift. It usually takes 12 to 18 months for them to fall into the new routine. In some cases, it can even take clients 24 months to warm up to the new system.

However, the rhythm of a steady "paycheck" from their investments in their banking accounts eases the mental block. The difference is that instead of getting paychecks from companies where they worked, they now get paychecks from companies where they invested.

This consistent income helps ease initial fears and empowers them to embrace their retirement years confidently. I also encourage them along the way. For example, at first, they may cut back and stay home. If this is the case, I begin to ask them about vacations. Do they want to travel? They often respond with, "Well, I don't know. I'm a little nervous because I'm not working."

"Why don't you start with a staycation in your city or something else small, like a camping trip?" I ask them.

As funny as it might sound, the aim is to gradually spend more money until you reach the amount you can comfortably spend.

If you want to take a big trip but are anxious about the cost, break it down into smaller pieces. This was the case for Jim. I encouraged him to think about the small things he could do to accomplish this goal. Where did he want to go and do? Did he know how much it would cost, or need help getting a quote?

We set a time to book the trip and turn it into a concrete plan. The goal wasn't to spend money for the sake of spending money. The goal was instead to spend money where it counts to enjoy life and do the things he always wanted to do. We set a deadline of two weeks for his decision-making process so he wouldn't get stuck in perfectionism.

Small steps can help move beyond financial impasse, but there are other ways you can get unstuck as well. If you find yourself avoiding something because of the cost, such as turning on lights at night outside even though you would like to, working through the actual cost by yourself or with someone else can be helpful. How much does a high-efficiency LED light bulb cost? How much would it cost to have the light on for the desired length? Running the light four hours a day could cost three cents a year. Is the juice worth the squeeze? Sometimes, you're giving something a lot of effort, but you're trying to squeeze juice out of a rock.

Another thing you can try is sharing experiences. For example, say your daughters are graduating from college and about to launch into adult careers and lives. One of your long-term goals is to travel to Spain, so you could offer to fund a family trip. This way, it becomes a family bonding opportunity and a chance to create lasting memories together. You get to enjoy time with your daughters while doing something you've always wanted to do.

Even with these strategies, it can be helpful to seek assistance. A good financial planner can help ease these fears. One of my jobs as a financial planner is to help people so they don't have to worry about their finances. If someone pushes their spending envelope too far, I help rein them in. I let my clients know if we are going out of bounds.

Sometimes clients need extra help, and a licensed therapist or mental health professional is better able to address some of their financial issues. This is especially true if the issue touches multiple areas of their lives or has its roots in traumatic experiences. And guess what? We build therapy into their retirement budget until they feel they no longer need it.

CHAPTER 30 REVIEW

- Some people are panicked by the transition to living off savings and pensions and will stop most spending altogether.
- If you are gripped by this anxiety and find yourself unable to spend money, here are approaches that help:
    - Set up an automatic transfer from your invested funds to your checking account once a month. This can act like a "paycheck" and help ease the transition to retirement.
    - Identify a goal you want to reach but have been reluctant to pursue due to money fears. Break it into smaller, more manageable steps with a backstop date so you don't get caught up in making everything "perfect".

- Break down the cost savings that you are accumulating through your actions. Are they truly worthwhile, or are you trying to wring water from a stone?
- Share if you don't want to spend the money just on yourself. For example, if you want to go to Spain but feel selfish about spending money, share the trip with someone you love.
- If you need help and confidence, it can help you find a financial planner you trust who can act as a sounding board and safety net. If that isn't sufficient, consider therapy with a licensed practitioner to help move you toward your happiest retirement.

CHAPTER 30 DISCUSSION QUESTIONS

1. Have you stopped spending? If so, how is that playing out in your current life?

2. Did any of the strategies I outlined above seem particularly helpful in moving past your financial lockdown? Make a plan below to implement the strategy and set a date on the calendar so you can evaluate its effectiveness.

CHAPTER 31

From Splurge to Strategy—Managing Binary Thinking and Intentional Spending

RELATED TO FINANCIAL lockdown, I also frequently see binary thinkers. Binary thinkers, or as I like to call them, sporadic splurgers, are people who have been very controlling with money until they hit a point and spend a lot of money all at once.

Don't try to spend money on everything at once. If you aren't used to spending money, you might accidentally spend a lot more than you expect, and it will add up. It can start with overspending on hobbies, then more on kitchen renovation, car upgrades, and suddenly, a boat is in the driveway.

I recommend setting a fund or an "I'm allowed to do this" budget for these clients. Whether it's $1,000 or $100 a month, your objective is to spend that money on something you enjoy.

For example, you can take a yoga class if you want to. Try a few different yoga schools and see how much they cost elsewhere. Once you select a place you enjoy and decide how many classes you would like to take, start automatically transferring the set amount of yoga money monthly. It will remind you that you need to take that class this month.

Pace yourself as you go and spend money only in one area at a time. Then, as you adjust to the new pace of spending and its impact on your bank account, you can fine-tune appropriately.

CHAPTER 31 REVIEW

- Binary thinkers or sporadic splurgers are people who have been very controlling with money until they spend a lot of money all at once. This can lead to spending more money than anticipated.
- For people with this tendency, I recommend setting a "I'm allowed to do this" budget, which they are encouraged to spend on a steady basis.
- Pace yourself and choose areas to spend money on to allow you to adjust your spending pace and its impact.

CHAPTER 31 DISCUSSION QUESTIONS

1. Are you a sporadic splurger? Are there any ways that you see this quality as needing balance in your life?

2. Activity: Money Journal
   a. Set up your journal: Choose a method for recording your entries, such as a physical notebook, a

note-taking app on your phone, or a dedicated document on your computer.

b. Record each spending event: Each time you spend money, note the following:
    1. Setting: Where were you? (e.g., Target, scrolling TikTok in bed)
    2. Planned purchase: What did you intend to buy? (e.g., toilet paper, groceries, a dress for an upcoming wedding)
    3. Pre-spending emotion: How were you feeling before you made the purchase?
    4. Post-spending emotion: How did you feel after buying it?
    5. Planned vs. Actual: Did you buy what you planned? How much did you plan to spend vs. how much did you spend?
    6. Company: Was anyone with you when you made the purchase?
c. Keep this journal for at least two to three weeks, recording every time you spend money.
d. Reflect on how these patterns might connect to past financial experiences you identified in your Money Timeline. Are your present emotions or belief patterns similar to those from your past?

____

____

____

____

e. Consider next steps based on what you've learned from your journal and any changes you'd like to make. What strategies can you implement to align your spending more closely with your values and goals?

CHAPTER 32

Wealth Without Shame—How to Embrace Your Financial Success in Retirement

SOME CLIENTS FEEL ashamed of their wealth, especially if their friends and/or family circle aren't wealthy. It can be awkward if someone wants to go on a trip with their friends but prefers to stay at a Four Seasons while their friends stay at the Red Roof Inn down the street.

While awkward, it is okay to be wealthy. If these feelings hold you back from doing something you want, a gracious way to bridge the gap is to magically have an "extra" of whatever you want to do. "Hey, I'm going to this concert, and I have an extra ticket!" is one example. Alternatively, you can invite people along. "We're getting an Airbnb and renting a house for the family. Everyone else shows up, okay?" This can alleviate social anxiety while allowing all of you to have the experiences you always dreamed of.

Philanthropy offers another way to navigate complicated feelings around wealth. If you donate to one or more charities during your working years, there is no reason to stop in retirement (unless you don't want to anymore).

If charitable donations aren't a part of your financial picture yet, retirement provides an excellent opportunity to start. Pick one or two organizations that speak to you as meaningful causes. You can feel good about spreading your wealth by donating a reasonable amount to them monthly or annually. You can also give money to specific endeavors, like the grandkids' college funds or supporting local businesses.

It can also help to look at your life from a broad perspective. If you're a business owner, you created jobs and enabled countless families to live a good life. You contributed to the economy by driving business development and investing in your company.

Enjoy what you've earned. You deserve to take lavish vacations if you want to. You should have a country club membership if that's your thing. Enjoy eating at gourmet restaurants? Yes, that should be something you allow yourself to do as well. It is okay to be wealthy. Embrace the opportunities to use that money for good, including for yourself.

CHAPTER 32 REVIEW

- Wealth can create complicated feelings in people, particularly if their wider circle doesn't have the same wealth.
- One gracious way to bridge this gap is to have a magical extra of whatever you want to share, such as a concert ticket or an extra room at an Airbnb. Then, you can involve your loved ones while still getting to do what you want.
- Philanthropy is another way to manage wealth guilt. Choose a cause that aligns with your values and donate to it regularly.
- Take a wide lens. Throughout your career, you likely helped many people in many ways, from the direct impact of your actions to the jobs you created. It is time for you to enjoy your wealth.

CHAPTER 32 DISCUSSION QUESTIONS

1. Are you struggling with wealth guilt? How does that impact your life today?

2. If so, did any strategies for managing wealth guilt resonate with you? Write a plan to implement them below.

PART 6

Getting Unstuck When Making Decisions

FINANCIAL ANXIETIES AREN'T the only things that can hold up decision-making. Other areas and tendencies can create unexpected roadblocks to your ideal retirement.

These roadblocks can be created by personality types, generate overwhelming feelings, and lead to broad cognitive distortions that permeate and hinder decision-making.

CHAPTER 33

Feelers vs. Planners—Two Different Approaches to Decision-Making

A FEW YEARS later, Martha and Timothy were back in my office. Timothy was very excited about an opportunity to invest in a second property near Lake Tahoe, one of their favorite family vacation spots. "We found the perfect cabin. It's the right size, overlooks the lake, and several rental management companies are in the area. We can make our money back on the house as a rental, everything is taken care of, and it'll be a place to call home when we visit," he enthused.

Martha was more hesitant. "Sure," she started. "It does sound nice, but we didn't make our plan around getting another home. The property looks nice, but we haven't researched enough to know if this will pay off in the long term."

They were stuck and wanted me to weigh in. This scenario is common. I often see couples frozen between two decision-making approaches: Feelers and Planners.

Feelers tend to adopt a more reactive approach to decision-making. One aspect of their decision-making is that when encountering a roadblock or unexpected change in circumstances, they are more likely to rapidly adjust their plans or change direction to accommodate the new reality. This ability to adapt quickly is valuable, especially when there are many changes and new challenges. However, when left unchecked, this reactive tendency can lead to emotion-based or impulsive decision-making instead of decisions centered on long-term goals.

For example, a Feeler may see an opportunity to invest in an exciting, new stock or business venture. The instinct to capitalize on an exciting opportunity may be strong. They might invest heavily in a rush because of their feelings. This could lead them to overlook more calculated or strategic decisions, like ensuring their portfolio is well distributed or weighing the larger context surrounding the stock or business venture. This emotion-based approach can be more flexible, but Feelers can jump into decisions without taking the time to analyze risks or long-term implications.

In retirement planning, this tendency to react to short-term impulses can manifest as changing spending habits or making large, unplanned purchases when emotions are high. For instance, a Feeler might splurge on a vacation or an expensive purchase like a second house or a luxury car on a whim. Alternatively, they may avoid adjustments if it doesn't spark their emotional interest. While these decisions might feel satisfying at the moment, they may not always align with the broader financial goals or the stability that the Feeler wants to achieve long term.

Conversely, Planners tend to take a more structured approach to decision-making. True to their nickname, they focus on the plan and hold steady during short-term fluctuations or rapid changes. Rather than making quick decisions based on immediate circumstances or feelings, Planners take their time to gather information, assess options, evaluate long-term outcomes, and mull it over—no matter how long it takes. They want to be sure they are making the best decision possible. This patient, methodical approach allows them to make well-informed decisions, but it can also lead to challenges if unchecked.

The Planner's tendency to wait for and gather evidence before taking action can sometimes result in missed opportunities. Instead of jumping on a fast-moving opportunity, making quick adjustments is necessary. Planners may be so focused on sticking to a particular retirement savings goal that they fail to adjust when unexpected expenses arise, such as a change in the cost of living. Planners tend to get locked into analysis paralysis about decisions as simple as purchasing a new toaster oven.

The desire to follow a strict, predetermined path can sometimes lead to rigidity even when circumstances change. For example, a Planner may have a schedule they strictly follow daily. If Planners are unwilling to change, they could limit their opportunities to try new things, like classes or volunteer work, and restrain their social circles. Additionally, it may make it difficult to respond to new circumstances, such as a health concern.

Both Feelers and Planners possess invaluable personality traits. Feelers respond quickly to change and adapt to new situations. Planners thoroughly consider decisions and explore options patiently before they set sail. The strongest results happen when Feelers and Planners borrow traits from one another for a steadier and more balanced approach.

Feelers can benefit from taking a moment to step back and thoroughly consider things before making significant decisions. They can discuss the action and its potential results with a friend or other loved one who is a Planner, or meet with an industry professional like a financial planner. They could create a specific account for discretionary expenses or establish a cooling-off period before making significant decisions. By building an intentional space between impulse and action, Feelers can have the capacity to make more thoughtful decisions that align with their broader goals and values.

Alternatively, Planners benefit when they introduce more flexibility into their decision-making process. This doesn't mean abandoning their long-term goals or process, but allowing more life to happen within their broader plans. One way that Planners can do that is to create set days throughout the year to reassess their goals, the performance of their current plans and structure, and the context of their circumstances. This can give them the ability to make changes that are aligned with their evolving needs and situations. Planners can also develop their ability to make more minor, incremental adjustments along the way instead of waiting for the "perfect" moment or the "right" amount of data by checking in with others when considering making significant decisions.

The key for both Planners and Feelers is to embrace their natural strengths while allowing growth. For Feelers, this means embracing their emotional awareness and adaptability while accepting more structure and space for decision-making. For Planners, it involves accepting their patience and stick-to-it-iveness while allowing more adaptability and responsiveness. Both types of decision-makers can create a healthy balance by fostering growth and nurturing their strengths.

These two personality approaches to decision-making can cause bumps in the process, particularly between couples. However, these competing personality types aren't the only barriers to decision-making. Another issue that causes decision-making hiccups across personalities is overthinking.

CHAPTER 33 REVIEW

- There are two common decision-making approaches: Feelers and Planners.
- Feelers take a more reactive approach to decision-making, which helps them rapidly adjust their plans but can also lead to more impulsive decisions.
- Planners take a more structured approach to decision-making, which helps them hold steady and make thorough decisions but can also lead to rigidity.
- The strongest results are when Feelers and Planners borrow from one another.

CHAPTER 33 DISCUSSION QUESTIONS

1. Are there any decisions that you're stuck on? What exactly is the parameter of the decision?

2. Are you a Feeler or a Planner?

3. How has that influenced your decisions in the past?

4. How does that help and hinder you when it comes to making decisions?

CHAPTER 34

Overthinking—The Hidden Barrier to Decision-Making

ONE OF THE most common causes of stuck decisions is overthinking. This often occurs when there are too many options or too much information, making a decision feel more complex and overwhelming than necessary. In these situations, the mind tends to meticulously grip onto every detail, process, and outcome until it is frozen. It grinds to a halt under the sheer mental load and the friction of anxiety. When our brains overthink, it leads to avoidance, as the path forward becomes less clear.

There can be several reasons behind overthinking. Usually, it's because the person is too involved in the details and is confusing themselves (looking at you, Planners!). Overthinking can lead to heavy research and constant churning over options, leading to analysis paralysis. This often spurs people to defer the decision more and more until they're stuck in a procrastination loop. The overwhelming number of choices can cause someone to shut down when considering the different options.

Another reason is the paradox of choice. If there are 300 types of shampoos in the shampoo aisle, which one do you choose? Companies create niche shampoos (dry, dandruff, etc.) so that by the time you're walking out of the aisle, you're buying three types for three different scenarios. Or, for the true overthinker, perhaps you are buying one of each shampoo to try them all.

The first step is to acknowledge that you're facing an overthinking problem. Generally, you realize this when you can't decide on an essential topic after constantly circling the issue or perhaps avoiding something that needs to be addressed. This recognition usually means you're focusing on the wrong details.

Once you've realized you are stuck, looking at the big picture is one way to get unstuck. What are you trying to achieve? Step back, examine these motivations, and become oriented toward the best solutions. If it helps, write down the big picture or discuss it with someone you trust. Once you've narrowed in on your goal, home in on it so it is specific. You may want to write down your specific goal and put it somewhere visible whenever you think about the decision. This will help you stay focused amidst the noise.

Your goal might be to minimize taxes, but for whom and when? Are you trying to reduce taxes for yourself or what your loved ones will inherit down the road? Sift out your priorities so you can understand what needs to come first.

If you have competing priorities, you can also consider whether you need an all-or-nothing solution. Many solutions can be buffet style, where you pick and choose a bit of each element of consideration to balance things out. If you opt for this decision style, remember which things combine well and in what order. It's just like going to Golden Corral. It's okay if the gravy gets onto the meat, but not if it goes on the cake, and if you get dessert with your main course. Do you want to listen to the grandkids and do what they want (which will probably be to get the dessert first), or do you want to do something else?

Alongside staying focused, it's also essential to keep things in perspective. Changing a flight path by two degrees may result in a radically different destination, but that is far less likely to happen with most decisions you'll make. For most decisions, however, there are many opportunities to look out the window, see that you've gone slightly off course, and adjust your headings. If you invest in the wrong stock today, you'll have a chance to sell it and buy something better in the future. If you move to the wrong house, nothing will keep you there. You can recover from mistakes.

CHAPTER 34 REVIEW

- One of the most common causes of stuck decisions is overthinking. This often happens when there are too many options or too much information.
- The first step is to realize that you're stuck overthinking a problem. If this is the case, take a step back and look at the big picture to include the significance of the situation and your priorities.

- If you have competing priorities, consider whether you need an all-or-nothing solution or can customize things to suit your needs.
- Keep things in perspective. Consider the decision's actual importance and whether you'll be able to correct the course if needed.

CHAPTER 34 DISCUSSION QUESTIONS

1. Have you been stuck in overthinking? If so, explore below the decision you are stuck in and what is behind your overthinking (e.g., too many options).

2. If you are stuck overthinking a problem, write the overall problem using the big picture. Does looking at the problem from the big picture change your approach?

3. Is there another way you can compromise between your competing priorities in this problem to better meet your needs?

CHAPTER 35

The Hidden Costs of FOMO—How the Fear of Missing Out Impacts Decisions

TOO MANY OPTIONS and too much information don't just lead to overthinking. They can lead to other challenges as well. When combined with social pressure, I often see people get stuck in the mucky swamp known as fear of missing out (FOMO).

FOMO initially referred to the social-based fear that one was missing out on or not being included in social events or situations, and usually stems from too much information about what other people are doing or, more precisely, what it seems like other people are doing. Social media intensified this anxiety for many as we became immersed in all of the interesting and exciting things other people are doing, nearly instantaneously.

FOMO can extend to other parts of our lives, though. In retirement, it can look like the fear of missing out on trending health schemes and diets. It can be particularly salient in finances because there are always new technologies, materials, and companies that people are running after. It feels very urgent because one doesn't want to miss out on any significant financial opportunity.

Take the rise of Bitcoin. When its value skyrocketed, many investors rushed in because of FOMO. It was the hip thing to do, and nobody wanted to miss the train. By doing so, many ended up buying high and selling low. That is usually because Bitcoin is generally at its peak value when a trend is reported.

This highlights an important point: timing is everything in investing. If you act on rumors or hype, you are at significant risk of responding to the tail end of a trend rather than its beginning. If everyone is talking about it, the market is probably overheated and could be nearing a correction (aka downturn). If you're hearing about a fresh investment from someone who is not a professional—say a cashier at your local grocery store—the bubble may be about to burst, and investing in the trending item could lead to financial losses.

It is crucial to keep things in perspective when dealing with FOMO, particularly on social media. People only post and share the shiny parts of their lives. If it is good, it goes onto the newsfeed. If it's only half-good, the good half will be shared for people to "like." The bad halves and the altogether rotten parts don't usually make it to people's profile pages or into our conversations. If an acquaintance claims to have uncanny gut feelings about stocks and urges you to invest heavily in a new company because they have made money in the past that way, it is good to take it with a grain of salt. Perhaps it did lead to profits last time, but the time before that? Maybe not.

CHAPTER 35 REVIEW

- Fear of missing out refers to the social-based fear of missing out on or not being included in events, trends, opportunities, and more.
- FOMO usually stems from too much information about what other people are doing or, more precisely, what it seems like other people are doing.
- FOMO can spur people to invest in trendy but ultimately unprofitable ventures and stocks.
- When managing feelings of FOMO, keep things in perspective. People only post their successes and sometimes inflate how well things are going. Take everything with a grain of salt.

CHAPTER 35 DISCUSSION QUESTIONS

1. Does FOMO affect the way you spend your time and money? Are you happy with its current impact?

CHAPTER 36

Recognizing TINA—How All-or-Nothing Thinking Limits Your Choices

WHILE INFORMATION ABOUT our friends and neighbors and social pressure can lead to FOMO, which can steer our decisions awry, too much of a specific type of information can lead to another fallacy called "there is no alternative" (TINA).

TINA, which is similar to the extremist thinking that we discussed in the previous chapter, is based on an all-or-nothing perspective that makes people feel like they are strapped onto the front of a runaway train. For example, a recent retiree could join a particular living situation and feel like there is no way to change it. "I have to live in a condo at this particular location. I paid a ridiculous deposit, and my son lives a few blocks away. My son isn't talking to me right now, but I have to live here in case things change. There is no alternative!"

This feeling can even extend to the breed of dog they own. "I have always owned Yorkies and only Yorkies for the past 30 years. It's the only dog breed I could consider owning!" There is almost no limit to the things people can get stuck on, from how they dress to the car they drive.

This can play a profound role in finances when people think there is only one correct option, despite what others, particularly seasoned professionals, tell them. For example, they may completely dismiss bonds because they don't offer a high return, even though bonds can serve as an essential safety net and buffer within a well-rounded portfolio. Or they will say they only buy stocks on Tuesdays because once they get an excellent stock deal, they lose opportunities and income because of their dogged insistence that the only day to buy stocks is Tuesdays.

TINA is based on the assumption that current market conditions or trends will continue forever. This is known as recency bias, which prioritizes current market conditions over historical ones and can cloud your judgment. It can make you believe that a good thing will always be good or that a bad situation will always remain bad. Both of these can obfuscate good decision-making.

It's easy to rely on the familiar as you approach retirement age, but this time can also be an opportunity to explore new hobbies and activities. Recognizing when you're stuck can be challenging, but leaning on a friend or loved one can help you identify where you're hindered in TINA.

Once you identify an area of TINA, focus on identifying the contours of your belief (e.g., "I will never move out of this house") and explore it further. Why do you feel like you will never move out of this house? What does the house mean to you? Is there something like your independence that you heavily connect with this place? Would you live in this house even if it means you're more socially isolated and financially restrained? What if you had a major health crisis and required advanced long-term care? Exploring these aspects of your TINA belief can help you understand it better and see the potential scenarios when you may have to abandon it altogether.

CHAPTER 36 REVIEW

- There is no alternative (TINA) is based on an all-or-nothing perspective and assumes that the current conditions or trends will continue forever.
- In investments, TINA appears when people assume current market trends will continue forever. In life, TINA shows that people only do the same things.
- If an area of your life is stuck in TINA, identify the contour of your belief and explore it so you can understand it better and work through potential scenarios to move past it.

CHAPTER 36 DISCUSSION QUESTIONS

1. How does TINA thinking creep into your life? Can you see it holding you back?

CHAPTER 37

Breaking Down Big Decisions—A Simple Framework for Clarity

IF YOU STILL feel overwhelmed when facing a big decision, there is more you can do to alleviate your anxiety and find a way forward. Decision-making can be daunting and overwhelming, but breaking the decision into its key components will help bring clarity and clear thinking back into the decision-making process. These components are as follows:

1. Description
2. Aims
3. Whom it effects
4. When it must be decided
5. Impact

First, you will identify a description of the decision you need to make. Condense the decision down to one or two sentences. Consider what is at the core of your decision and why it matters. The key point of this exercise is to break it down to its most essential elements and keep it at a high level. You want to home in on what you need to decide and its most critical components without getting bogged down in the details, which can distract from the big picture. Try your best to stick to regular sentences if you're using semicolons or writing in run-on sentences (which, for clarity, we'll consider cheating in this exercise). The result is a streamlined and concise description of your decision that breaks down the essence of your choice.

When you have the core component of your decision in front of you, dig into your decision further to identify the aims of your decision. What are you trying to accomplish, for whom, and when? It's easy to get lost in vague and indecisive terms, so specificity is key, and the more straightforward your objective, the more precise your path will be. Consider whether you are trying to solve a problem, achieve a goal, or do something else. With the main objective in hand, consider for whom it is essential: yourself, family, friends, or community?

Once you have pinpointed the aims, you need to identify whom it affects. Understanding whom your decision impacts will help you understand the stakes of the decision. It can also help determine whether other people must be involved in decision-making.

When does the decision need to take place, and when will the impacts be felt? If the timing is imminent, you will have less flexibility to explore and consider other options and you'll need to prioritize this decision. Those three elements—what, who, and when—will help guide your decision and how much you should prioritize it. Get as specific as you can about what you're trying to do. This will help you set the parameters around your decision-making process.

Lastly, think about the impact of your decision. Is it as significant as it feels? Will this decision have rippling effects across other areas, or is it isolated? How long will the decision's impact be felt? For more tangible aspects of the decision, this can be a good time to reach out to a professional for a quote to weigh the financial impact of your decision, like a realtor on the costs of houses. Are there any relationship impacts? Understanding the impact of your decision can help you keep things in perspective, especially if fear and anxiety continue to hold you back.

Breaking down the decision into these elements will help you build a clear framework. One clear path may make itself known through this process, or you may find that a few solutions are the best. If one path doesn't immediately emerge as the best solution, write out all the alternative solutions and put a deadline on your calendar for when you need to decide. Think about it when you have the time, do more research if needed, and then decide on the deadline date.

This framework helped Martha and Timothy as they debated the second home. Timothy felt very strongly about the house, while Martha wanted to learn more about the financial consequences and feasibility before they launched into the decision.

Working together on the decision definition was trickier than they initially anticipated, but they finally landed on the following:

- Concise description: We must decide whether to invest in this property next to Lake Tahoe.
- Aim: Evaluate and purchase a second property to be a vacation destination and a source of rental income.
- Whom it affects: Ourselves (vacation destination, rental income, and cost) and our children (vacation destination and possible inheritance).
- When we need to decide: In the next three months, before the historical Lake Tahoe annual housing price increases.
- Impact: Our portfolio, potentially diverting from steadier investments, time spent overseeing the purchasing and managing through agencies, and damage to the house and property from renters. More of a medium-term impact (5 to 10 years) before the house will likely pay itself off, even with the rental income, due to taxes. Possibly a good investment.

After we hashed out these elements during their visit, I gave them a list of homework to help them decide. Timothy and Martha interviewed realtors in the area that week and asked for some house quotes. They planned to visit in the next month to look at houses, interview management companies, and enjoy a short vacation. Timothy also found a friend who owned a similar vacation property he rented out through an agency. He set up a video call with him so he and Martha could learn more about the stresses and joys of owning another property.

This took effort and time from Martha and Timothy, but they had the time to do it and ended up enjoying the process. Timothy provided most of the energy for the process and conducted interviews while Martha researched options and background. They leveraged the strengths of each other as a Planner and Feeler, respectively, while they moved closer to their predetermined decision date.

When they returned to my office a month later, they were excited and relieved to tell me their decision. After finding a rental agency they were excited about, they decided to buy a condo instead of a house. It was a perfect compromise that minimized financial risk while still jumping on the opportunity to own a slice of their vacation heaven.

CHAPTER 37 REVIEW

- Breaking down tough and/or big decisions falls into the following steps:
    1. Description
    2. Aims
    3. Whom it effects
    4. When it must be decided
    5. Impact
- If you are making this decision with other people, such as a significant other, leverage your strengths to make the best decision possible.

CHAPTER 37 DISCUSSION QUESTIONS

1. If you are stuck on a decision:

    - Condense the problem to one or two sentences.
    - What specifically are you trying to accomplish?
    - Whom does it impact?
    - When does this decision need to happen and when will it take effect?
    - What is the impact of the decision?

2. If you completed the previous exercise, what did you learn from it? Brainstorm ideas below that meet your aims but minimize negative impacts. If necessary, take a break before filling in this exercise to allow maximum creativity.

PART 7

Making Plans for Aging with Dignity

JIM AND JOYCE returned to my office a few years later. They had been settling into their retirement lives well and had adjusted to post-career life. They had visited many places, including Japan, South Korea, and Norway, and planned a memorable trip with their two children to Mexico City next fall.

While they looked forward to their adventures, their next few conversations with me were difficult but necessary. Jim was now in his 70s. It was time to get serious about setting up their estate and aging plans. They had resisted setting up these appointments for a few years, but they were necessary for themselves and the children's sake.

As we settled across from one another, I jokingly said, "Well, this will be a cheerful discussion about death, aging, and taxes!" They eased a bit as we broke into an important but challenging topic.

Like many retirees, you may struggle to attend the meeting Jim and Joyce had with me that day. It is hard to work past the mental and emotional hurdles that surround aging and death. It can bring misconceptions. Before I help navigate documents like financial wills and trusts, I'd like to cover some vital ground: what advanced age can look like, choosing a caretaker, and how to communicate their plans to their loved ones. While these topics are tough, tackling them head-on will empower you and minimize headaches and heartache later.

CHAPTER 38

Assumptions Versus Reality—The Hard Truth About Aging and Care

SOMETIMES, PEOPLE UNDERVALUE the importance of *planning* to age with grace and dignity. It can be difficult to conceptualize the profound physical, mental, and emotional changes that occur as they reach advanced years, which is why one important question I often ask is, "Have you ever taken care of a parent, grandparent, or loved one who had medical issues?" Some of my clients have, and if so, they are usually more prepared to dive into their own long-term care plan. If not, my client's perspective can be unrealistic.

However, things get messy when someone faces advanced age without a plan. This is especially true in cases of memory decline. They don't understand what is happening, and they feel gaslit. In these situations, the things children and other loved ones do to support them are easily misinterpreted. For example, a loved one can try to hire much-needed help, to which the ailing person may say, "I don't need this. Who's this housekeeper person? It costs $30! Don't clean my bathroom!"

In these situations, the caretaker has to find ways within the family dynamic to determine who can get them to take action on a necessary item and who can't. The caretaker has to navigate when the person is having a good day, what they remember, and whether they are fulfilling their responsibilities.

Meanwhile, who controls their finances and can help them make medical decisions? What options do their loved ones have if they resist going anywhere while suffering? If they can't decide because they have cognitive decline, because they're in pain, or just had surgery, who can help them?

It's like being at a batting cage where you swing at every pitch. You'll miss some and hit others. This situation can lead to much anxiety for everyone involved and patchwork care.

Having one or two trusted individuals as your financial and medical powers of attorney can make a tremendous difference in your care and your loved ones' experience. It creates a safety net which, while it might not work perfectly, provides support during a crucial period.

Many who haven't experienced adult caretaking firsthand are dismissive of the realities of aging. They might say something vague like, "I'll just stay with my daughter," with a wave of their hand. Some people, especially younger and healthier people, have to grow into thinking about advanced age. They don't see it happening if they have never experienced it.

When helping someone who denies or downplays the effects of aging, you can't push them. That approach typically leads to resistance. When the person dismissively tells me their daughter will manage their care, I ask follow-up questions.

- Will she watch you and make sure that you don't wander if you have dementia?
- Does she also have a child who needs to be taken to four different places because they're on baseball and travel soccer teams?
- Does your grandkid need to drop out of soccer because you need someone to watch you in case you burn down the house while making toast?
- Will she leave her job to watch you?
- Will she and her family be able to operate without her income?

Aside from the life realities of assuming that she or another child can care for you, many things can happen to your child. Perhaps they run into financial, health, or relationship issues, or could already be caring for another relative.

Continence and showering, which often trouble people during advanced age or illness, often ground people. Folks are usually fine with their kids taking care of them until it comes to bodily functions. "Wait, I changed their diapers. They ain't changing mine! We have a good relationship now and I don't want to soil it, literally!"

Sometimes, people stay at home slightly longer than they should until a health event forces them to move to a hospital or long-term care facility. Hopefully, when they go to a care facility, it isn't because of a major event involving severe danger, such as a house fire, car accident, bad fall, or losing money to scammers.

This was true for one client, who asked, "Can we just wait one more year to do this move?" Just a few days ago, she couldn't find her way home from her neighbor's house. She had lived in the same house for 40 years. Usually, when the kids and everyone say it's time, it should have been done 6 to 12 months ago. By the time the person voluntarily does it, it's often dangerous, and if you're in the car with them driving, you are doing the rosary or praying!

Besides moving into an assisted care or similar facility, discussing no longer driving is difficult. Obtaining a driver's license is often seen as a symbol of American freedom. As teens, most people are eager to get their permit. Suddenly, even though they've grown up and been driving for decades, people start getting their licenses taken away.

Eventually, you're not going to be able to drive. On that day, whom do you want to make that decision? Do you want someone to make that decision for you? Do you want it to be a point of contention in the family and lead to a blow-up event, or would you rather ease into it? Often, there are options that you can explore. I start to discuss this with clients who are in their early 70s. If they aren't able to drive, how are they going to get around? It might be beneficial to practice taking the shuttle bus. Try using Uber if you've never used it before. You can practice and confront some of these things just by doing it.

Even with these realities laid out before them, it takes time. It sometimes takes three to five years to get a client to make their advanced age care plans and prepare so things will go smoothly when the plan is implemented. Consistently reminding them and bringing it up a few times a year helps them make a plan and talk it through. It takes time to face it, and it is usually a gradual process for people to consider. Very rarely does it hit them in such a way that they say, "Oh, yeah, there is a chance that I may age slowly, and I need to make a plan for that today while I face my mortality."

Conversely, someone who has experienced the end-of-life aging process may over-prepare and constantly worry about it. Every aspect of the process consumes them, from care options to wills. For the latter, they may continuously update and tweak their estate plan. They want to be prepared, but it transforms into scratching an emotional itch.

The best spot to be is somewhere in the middle—well prepared while you still live in the present. Aging is tough, but this is life. It's important to consider how we can prepare for it and make sure that we age and die with dignity. Crucially, it's essential to consider your loved ones and how to create a scenario that works best for you and them.

CHAPTER 38 REVIEW

- Value the importance of planning to age with grace and dignity.
- It's not easy to conceptualize the profound physical, mental, and emotional shifts that happen as you reach advanced years unless you have experienced adult caretaking.
- When people resist or are dismissive about making a plan, it helps to gently test their assumptions with questions concerning their care, including who will take care of them and what will happen if that person is unavailable. It may take time to persuade someone to make a plan.
- Some who have experienced advanced adult care overprepare and constantly worry about their plans.
- The best place to be is somewhere in the middle, where you're prepared and living in the now.

CHAPTER 38 DISCUSSION QUESTIONS

1. How do you see aging? How do you think it will personally impact you?

____

____

____

____

____

____

____

2. What fears of aging do you have?

CHAPTER 39

Building Your Care Team—Who's in Your Family Circle?

When my clients and I discuss aging with dignity, I want to know, "Who will be in charge?" While this might seem simple, the answers are very personal. Aging brings many changes, from physical to emotional. It often requires help with day-to-day tasks and managing significant transitions.

If you need additional assistance, you want to know who will care for you. If you aren't sure, I recommend you consider people based on three criteria: relationship, bandwidth, and personality.

For relationship criteria, I recommend thinking about those in your family. Family matters even more as we age. Family can provide emotional support, care, and meaning when we are vulnerable.

Family has many definitions, but it comes down to who is most important to you. First, there are spouses and long-term romantic partners. These people are a significant part of our lives. Second, there are relatives: parents, siblings, children, nephews, nieces, and cousins. Third, some friends might qualify as family. These are the people you go on vacation with or whom you'd call in an emergency. If you can't remember whether you turned off a faucet, you could ask them to check your house. All of these people can fall under the nebulous network known as family.

As you consider people within your family, you must consider the quality of your relationship and connection with each person. How well do you communicate with them? Do you feel like the two of you are honest with one another? Would they respect your wishes, even if they didn't align with what they think is best? It is crucial that whomever you choose for this role is someone you can trust.

Bandwidth refers to who can take care of things and is able to handle additional responsibilities. Taking care of someone who is aging is a significant amount of work for an undetermined amount of time. How much capacity does this person have to take on additional responsibilities that wouldn't be devastating? Do they show through patterns of behavior that they can handle more complex tasks in general?

Finally, there is personality. Who in your family has the inclination to be caring and is patient enough to handle being a caretaker? Some people just are not built that way. Do they struggle with administrative tasks like medical billing, managing accounts, or talking to lawyers? Some people are wired better to be caretakers and meet these challenges than others, which is why personality is just as important as relationships and bandwidth.

There won't be a perfect person who flawlessly fills the relationship, bandwidth, and personality qualities. That is okay. The goal isn't to find the single ideal person. Think of this person as competent and someone who will handle most things well. Don't try to find "A" players because not everybody has them. You need to find somebody good enough to get the equivalent of a 3.0 student. A 3.0 isn't perfect, but it represents consistent effort and competency.

It doesn't have to be one person either. If you're struggling to fill the role, you can split responsibilities. You can have one person who fills more of a caretaker/medical role, while another person handles finance.

This division of labor addresses several problems when considering the list of potential future caretakers. It can also help balance challenges such as varying relationships, limited bandwidths, and/or differing personalities.

If you have multiple children, sharing responsibilities can also help alleviate some of the strain. For example, some children will offer help even though they've never lived completely alone. If they haven't been able to live independently, how could they take care of you? A reasonable solution might be giving that child some limited responsibility, such as helping you get to hospital appointments.

It might be that you don't have anyone to trust or help you at your most vulnerable, or to manage your assets after you pass away. When this happens, you can hire corporate trustees and money managers for your financials. Unfortunately, this is still a bit of a cottage industry where it's hard to find services if you have a lower net worth.

Either way, major health and care decisions must be handled by a close friend who can act as a medical proxy. It's important not to stack too much responsibility on friends, but they can approve medical procedures. There are court-appointed guardians if you can't find someone to fit this role. However, many find the idea of the state selecting someone to help you abhorrent.

It is essential to start thinking about who could help when you need it the most. Even before people reach the final stages of aging, they need loved ones around them who can check in and ensure they're doing okay. As you consider who might fill those roles, you can also think about how to help future caretakers by building strong systems.

As I worked with Jim and Joyce through these points during our initial meeting, we discussed their plan. Joyce intended to be Jim's primary caretaker if his health declined first and vice versa. After each other, they decided to put their eldest child, Nick, in charge of their financial and medical decisions. He lived nearby and was settling into his career. Their daughter, Alice, would be second on the list to make decisions after Nick. They planned to discuss this update with Nick the next week and then with Alice once they had Nick on board.

They left with a series of things they wanted more time to think about, particularly how they would determine when to stop driving. That was tough for Jim, who loved driving. They looked into options over the following weeks and tested different ideas. They were used to creative problem-solving—this was just another step along the path, and they knew they could manage it together.

CHAPTER 39 REVIEW

- Consider potential caretakers based on relationship, bandwidth, and personality criteria.
  - Relationship: People who are or are like family—consider the quality of your connection with them.
  - Bandwidth: People who can get things done, take care of things, and have the ability to handle additional responsibilities.
  - Personality: People with the inclination and patience to care for someone.
- No one will perfectly fulfill each quality. The aim is to find someone who is good enough. If no one person could fulfill this role in your life, consider splitting tasks between multiple people.
- If you have no one you consider family to assist you, you will need to identify a close friend who can act as a medical proxy just in case. If you can't find someone to fit this role, there are court-appointed guardians.
- For financial and legal support, you can use trusts and hire corporate trustees to handle all the finances, taxes, and legal scenarios if you have a higher net worth.

CHAPTER 39 DISCUSSION QUESTIONS

1. Whom would you consider part of your family, related and non-related?

2. Who are the strongest contenders to help you if you require advanced elderly care?

3. If no one is capable or available enough to serve as a possible caretaker, make a list of the services you require and start soliciting quotes and reviews for different services.

CHAPTER 40

Making Plans for Future Caretakers

IT'S BENEFICIAL TO support future caregivers early on before a significant health event occurs. It's unreasonable to expect someone to remain in one place to care for another until they pass away, whether that takes one year or 10. When do the breaks come? What's the backup plan?

Not too long ago, I had a client who said, "Oh, my son will do everything. That's why I have kids." When I asked her about showering and toileting, she replied, "Oh, no way!"

"Okay, do we need to have an aide come in?" I asked. We included that in the plan so the daughter could help and take her to appointments, but the line was drawn at personal hygiene.

If you can, start thinking through these ideas in advance. Don't be afraid to try them out and test out the issues along the way. Have an in-house aide come a few days a week. This will allow you to have the space and empowerment to make your own best decisions.

As you consider this advanced stage and decide the type of care you want and how you want it to be managed, it is also important to discuss it with the people you want to turn to for your advanced care.

CHAPTER 40 REVIEW

- Reflect on what kind of care you'd like to receive and what life might be like for your future caretakers. Consider what you would like them to take care of and what you'd like to hire someone to do.
- Consider how you can build in breaks for your caretakers. Discuss it with them in advance so they can make plans and vocalize their concerns.

CHAPTER 40 DISCUSSION QUESTIONS

1. Are there any struggles that you foresee potential future caretakers running into?

____

____

____

____

____

2. What values do you want your caretakers to consider if they need to make a significant health or financial decision on your behalf?

CHAPTER 41

Tackling Tough Talks—Preparing Your Loved Ones for Your Aging

CONFRONTING THE AGING process is challenging work for you and your loved ones. It's never fun and easy. However, if you can do it well, it can deepen relationships and strengthen families. Open, honest conversations with your loved ones can ease the aging process. The better the family dynamics, cooperation, communication, and love, the more dignified the aging process can be.

The best way to start this is through conversations with loved ones about your expectations and plans for aging. Being open about who is in charge of each role, your expectations, and how they will perform in those capacities eases anxiety and helps manage the transition process. The worst scenario is when there is no communication at all, which can lead to fighting, delayed care, and broken relationships.

As mentioned, however, talking about aging can be tough. Let them know in advance what you'll be discussing. Don't interrupt your family's conversation over the Thanksgiving table while they carve the turkey. That's not the time. It usually results in denial, especially from kids who say, "Mom, don't say that. That'll never happen to you. You'll be fine," or even "I don't want to talk about this." It can be challenging to manage, depending on how stubborn your child is.

Instead, set a separate time and let them know you need to get together to discuss legal and financial matters. You can then use the predetermined time to tell them everything in a thorough way. "Hey, I need to talk to you in case this were to happen. The legal documents are here. My advisor, CPA, and lawyers are here. These are the documents that you would need and these are your responsibilities."

You don't need to share financial information right away. Just let them know who is in which roles and where things can be found. Open communication should be balanced with sound common sense. Some people shouldn't be privy to certain information because they're not going to be involved—especially those who are bad with money or are suffering from issues like addiction.

Loved ones may struggle with your decisions for many reasons. For example, one of my clients had a daughter who was going through a divorce. While the daughter would've been an excellent choice to give their power of attorney, they decided not to choose her.

She was upset about being passed over for the responsibility. They broke the news in the best way possible, though, by saying, "You're going through a divorce right now, so in case something happens to us, your sister is going to handle things. She knows where everything is. This is not because we don't love you or trust you. It's because you're going through this, and we don't want to put more on you right now. That's the choice that we've made, and if you have any questions, let us know."

If and when the designated future caregiver is deeply in denial about your aging, I recommend practicing what I call "put it in the box." With this method, I suggest that once a year, my clients sit down with their loved ones for 15 to 30 minutes and make sure that they know where everything is and that things are up to date. This is to ensure everything's straight and everyone understands what is happening while allowing their loved ones to compartmentalize the discussion.

If you have decided on someone as your future caretaker and they say, "I can't handle it and I refuse to do it," don't just charge ahead. Talk to them and listen to what they have to say. If they are not able to serve, it is better to have an alternate in their place.

This is very important because when the primary person resigns, the person covering the gap has to use the power of attorney, resignation letters, and whatever else the state requires to acquire care for their loved one. This process creates crucial care delays.

If you know somebody can't serve as a potential caretaker, remove them from the list of actionable players. Move everybody else up the list and have replacements behind them. Keep a clean roster going, similar to what you might do if you were a football coach and were managing your quarterbacks. If they have surgery, they're not your quarterback anymore. Maybe next season they can play, but for now they're benched.

Communicating these plans is essential for you and your loved ones, even more so when someone else relies on you.

CHAPTER 41 REVIEW

- Discussing your aging plan can be difficult. Being open about who is in charge of each role, what your expectations are, and how they will be able to manage in those capacities eases anxiety and helps manage the transition process. The worst scenario is when there is no communication at all. This can lead to fighting, delayed care, and broken relationships.
- Designate a time in advance to discuss your aging and future care plan.
- While being open is helpful, you don't need to share every detail of your plan or current situation. Point them to the necessary people or information in case they need to step in.
- If one of your designated future caretakers is in denial about your aging, try the "put it in the box" method. This method involves a 15- to 30-minute annual chat with loved ones to ensure they know where everything is and that things are up to date.
- If someone refuses to be a potential caretaker or is no

longer suited for the role, remove them from the list, find an alternative, and communicate the changes to those involved.

CHAPTER 41 DISCUSSION QUESTIONS

1. What are the biggest challenges you see in communicating your care plans?

2. If you had to stop driving, what would be the best way to find out? Do you know how you would get about it?

CHAPTER 42

From Caregiver to Caregiver—Ensuring a Smooth Transition

SOMETIMES, IT'S ABOUT more than just us. Life throws many curveballs, and there may be someone who relies on you as a caregiver as you get older. This is very important for advanced special-needs children, elderly relatives, and others who require additional support and depend on you for their well-being and care.

If this is your situation, you need to restart the caretaker selection process but with this person in mind. Carefully consider who could step up to take your role. Just like you have to say, "Well, who would take care of me?" You have to decide who the person behind you will be.

Once you have decided who will take care of your loved one if and when you become incapacitated, it is the same process to make sure that they are ready, know where things are, and have a predetermined roster of who's next in line. Additionally, it's important to inform the responsible person in charge if and when something goes wrong.

If you are the last person standing, making a contingency care plan becomes problematic, but it is still achievable. You will have to look for professional services that can fill the role for that person. One area that can be particularly challenging is finding daily money managers. To find a quality one, look at the cost and scope of services offered and ask for references. It's like screening any other professional services—you then use these categories to choose one that you feel will be the best fit.

If you have to set up professional services, make sure that there are powers of attorney in place so those services can be replaced if they need to be switched out for whatever reason. Make sure that somebody has the power to do that, preferably without court action, although it's sometimes unavoidable. Discuss details with a lawyer who can provide sound advice relevant to your state and situation so you can continue to provide the best care to the most vulnerable people in your life.

Once you have a plan, practice it to ensure it works. When you notice one of your tires has low air pressure, you can wait until it blows out and you're stranded on the highway, or you could pull over and put some air in it, or call AAA before you're on the side of the road. Rehearsing contingency plans is essential when you provide care for a person with special needs, a mental illness, or drug issues. It has to be thought out for them because they probably can't do it themselves.

CHAPTER 42 REVIEW

- If you are a caretaker, carefully consider who could step up to take your role if necessary, weighing the same considerations outlined in Chapter 39.
- If you are the last person available to provide care, you will have to look for professional services that can fill your role. One area that can be particularly challenging is finding daily money managers. To find a quality one, look at the cost and scope of services offered and ask for references.
- If you have to set up professional services, make sure that there are powers of attorney in place to replace those services if they need to be switched out for whatever reason.
- Once you have a plan, practice it to ensure it works.

CHAPTER 42 DISCUSSION QUESTIONS

1. Is there anyone who relies on you for caretaking assistance? What kind of care do they require?

2. Make a list of possible caretakers who can step in for you. Make a plan to contact them to discuss the possibility and ensure they'd be open to fulfilling your role.

3. What information would need to be shared with the person filling in for you?

____

____

____

____

____

____

____

____

____

____

____

____

____

4. If no one is available to step in for you, list the services you need to identify. Then, make a plan below to solicit quotes and reviews for services and the legal and financial framework to support that plan.

____

____

____

____

CHAPTER 43

Collaborative Financial Planning—Teaching Kids to Own Their Future

IT IS NECESSARY to make plans for those who rely on you, but it is also helpful to prepare people who depend on you to a lesser extent. People usually face a broader dilemma: managing their children's relationship with money. They wonder whether they should financially support their children as adults, and, if so, how to navigate the conversation about the future.

When I help clients with children set up their wills and trusts, I ask them what their plan is with their kids. I ask, "Do you want your kids to get the whole $3 million right now with no guidance or restrictions?" Almost no one says yes, especially when children are in their mid-20s or younger.

Some kids need to learn the hard way—it's the only way they know. If you suspect your children fall into that category, there's good news: you can establish trusts to stop them from being their worst enemies. Trusts can prevent them from getting enough money upfront to support bad habits or decisions, or limit the damage.

Other legal structures also allow the gradual transfer of money to your kids to diminish the odds of them doing any damage to themselves with it. While this may be challenging to navigate, you can't support every whim, every business venture, or every major change during college.

Confidence in your children's ability to handle finances may change over time. If your kids are young when you retire, you may decide they're not ready to handle significant amounts of money. That could change if your kids were 18 when you retired, and 10 years later they have a steady job, a home, and a savings account for their retirement.

When people provide significant financial support to their adult children, discussing finances can help when they want to wean them off the financial aid. If you see a major event happening soon, test the backup plan. Tell them in advance so it's not a surprise. This conversation can start with something as simple as "I am 80 years old. Eventually, I'm going to die or go to a nursing home. The financial support is probably going to stop or shift. Let's start practicing what it would look like if this were different."

Establish a set dollar amount and have them start living as if that's all they will receive. Practice it and work out the kinks in advance so both of you can plan and make adjustments.

One of the healthiest ways to manage money with your children is collaborative coaching. Collaborative coaching means that you lead the conversation with questions, allowing your child to find their answers. Around the age when children can get their first job, have a brief discussion with them about financial concepts so they can learn how to be financially independent over time. It can help to go to a different place, like a reserved meeting room at the library, to ensure the conversation is taken seriously.

Figure 43.1

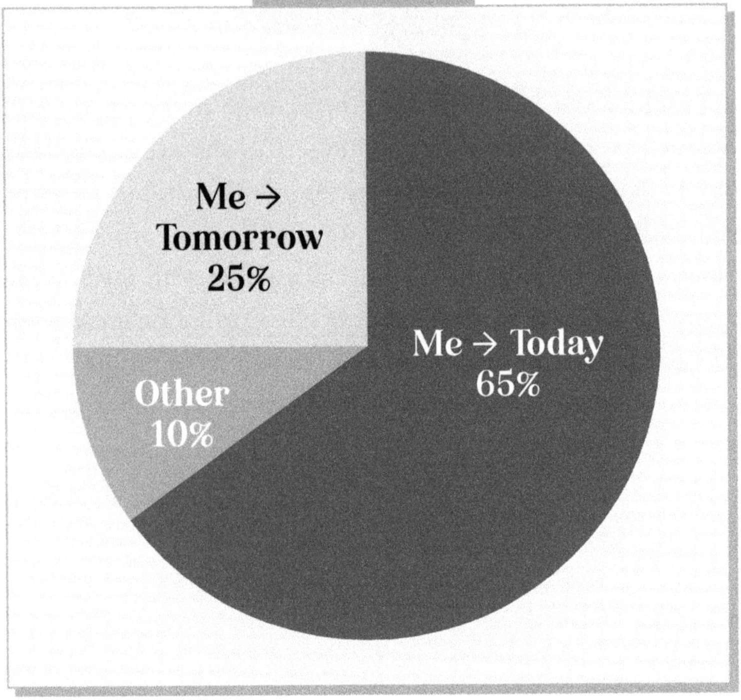

Help them make a "pie chart" budget, which involves setting aside money as it is earned for a specific purpose. You keep it very high-level and simple. For example, 30% of each paycheck should be set aside for emergencies or the future, 40% for their bills like audio streaming services, cell phone bills, etc., and the rest can be spent on anything they want. This establishes the habit of controlling money as it is earned, saving it, and planning for future spending.

As children get closer to finishing college or job training, this presents a natural opportunity to gradually introduce them to the real world and transition them to financial independence. Start discussing their future in concrete ways they can understand, such as asking what kind of apartment or house they want to live in, what town they would like to live in, and what they think it costs to live there.

Notice that I ask questions and don't tell them what they can and can't do. Part of being an adult is being able to self-regulate what you can and can't do and what you should and shouldn't do. Being told what they can and can't do may be the surest way to get a young adult to do the opposite!

I recently helped a client's son transition to financial independence. He had just finished graduate school and really wanted to live in Washington, D.C. My client was very concerned that it would be too expensive and that her son could not support himself. To find out, I asked the son where he thought he wanted to live in D.C., and what he thought it would cost to support himself there.

He said, "Well, I'm not sure, but I want to be there for job opportunities and I like the city life." I asked him to list what he thinks he would need to live there. He listed a place to live, food, and some spending money. "Okay, so no need for a car?" I asked him if he would like me to share a list of everyday items that some other client's children had as part of their living expenses from college in a big city. He filled in the list with dollar amounts based on what he found on internet searches about rent cost, cell phone plans, bus/uber/subway fares, medical insurance until he found a job, etc.

At the same time, he received a job offer. We calculated his take-home pay and found that he could live in D.C. on his salary but only go out once or twice a month. His parents were relieved that he would "be off the family payroll" and were willing to help him if something went wrong.

CHAPTER 43 REVIEW

- When people provide significant financial support to their adult children, a conversation about finances can help when they want to wean them off the financial aid.
- If you see a significant event happening soon, test the backup plan. Tell them in advance so it's not a surprise. Establish a set dollar amount and have them start living as if that's all they will get. Practice it and work out the kinks before you're forced to, so you both can plan and make adjustments.
- Teach your children through collaborative coaching how to keep a simple, high-level budget. I recommend making a "pie chart" budget and laying aside pre-designated income for different categories.
- Ask your adult children questions and let them come to their own decisions related to their money.

CHAPTER 43 DISCUSSION QUESTIONS

1. Do you have adult children who rely on you financially? Have you discussed the future of your financial support with them?

____

____

____

2. Do you need to practice the backup plan? What are some wrinkles that could arise? Can you raise your concerns with questions for your children in advance?

3. If you haven't discussed financial management with your children, make a plan below for discussing finances, particularly budgeting.

PART 8

Preparing and Communicating Estate Plans

A FEW YEARS back, I had a client named Anne. She divorced long ago and had two adult kids living in other states. She lived independently and didn't have an aging plan or a will. She helped her parents a little while they were aging, but didn't have to do much. She mostly just visited them in the nursing home over the holidays and wasn't involved in their care logistics or estate plans.

She was nervous about the topic of death (aren't we all?) and resistant to making a will. Eventually, we scheduled an appointment with me, her attorney, and her older daughter to complete her will at the attorney's office. In the first meeting, Anne answered the attorney's questions and decided how she wanted to structure her estate plan. However, at the next meeting, when she was supposed to sign the documents to make them effective, she froze and was afraid to sign the papers.

We scheduled another meeting to re-review everything and sign a few weeks later. She and I went through the documents together, discussed the plan again, and reassured her that signing a will doesn't mean you will imminently die, and that the documents can be amended if necessary. Eventually, we got it all done.

Just a few months after that, she slipped while mopping the kitchen floor and had a brain injury. She started to experience detrimental cognitive issues, including short-term memory loss. It began with her forgetting things, but it got worse and worse. She couldn't remember the day of the week, but she could go to the grocery store, buy stuff, and get home most of the time. Soon, though, the cognitive decline made it impossible for her to live on her own.

Her daughter asked me for help managing the transition, acknowledging the situation, and creating the medical power of attorney. She was able to make decisions on Anne's behalf, considering her mental decline.

This legal arrangement allowed her to make decisions on Anne's behalf and ensure that her wishes were still respected. Because of her rapid mental decline, the family chose to sell her house, which was filled with years of memories, and move Anne into an assisted living facility. Anne didn't want to move to either of the states where her children lived and wanted to maintain some level of independence. The assisted living facility was a good option for her, and she was very social there, even if she frequently reintroduced herself to fellow residents she had met before.

Even with the power of attorney, it was a hectic time for Anne's daughter and son. They lived in different states and struggled to ensure her bills were paid on time, mainly because she paid with checks. During her decline, she sometimes forgot to pay bills, which went to collections. To complicate things, her Social Security checks went to one bank account, but she spent her money from another. Anne's daughter, who had financial power of attorney, had to call the Social Security office to change the account information. Still, the Social Security office thought she was a fraudster and delayed the change, hampering her ability to help her mom.

As chaotic as it was, the situation unfolded relatively well. The legal documents were enforced before her fall and eventual memory decline. If those documents hadn't been in place, getting everything done would have been far messier. Even with these legal empowerments, it still took 12 months of concerted effort from us and her kids to get her positioned during her decline.

CHAPTER 44

Thinking About Dying and Death—Moving from Fear to Action

AGING IS HARD to plan for and confront as our bodies change and our roles shift. Death and dying can be even more difficult to conceptualize and accept, which can make it challenging to create plans.

Allow yourself a generous amount of grace. Confronting mortality is not something that can be resolved in a day—it's a long and complex journey filled with valid, difficult emotions, and this process looks different for everyone. It's hard to envision a future without being here or to imagine not seeing your great-grandkids.

Sometimes, people don't fear the dying process simply because they don't believe it will happen to them. They see themselves as being too young, healthy, and alive to consider the possibility. For others, this can take on a religious tone, as they say, "I have too much faith for that to happen." Some people are superstitious and think, "If I get my will done, I'll die." (No, you will only die if you don't get your will done and you cancel life insurance. That's what kills you!)

If you need motivation, picture the impact of not creating a plan for your loved ones. Imagine them putting their careers on hold, sabotaging their opportunities, and taking time away from their other loved ones because they have to take care of you for a year and a half. While they may begrudge the time they lose, imagine the additional stress and anxiety when there is no documentation to help ease and guide decisions and care provisions.

So even if you or your loved ones see the odds as low, let's just put something there. It doesn't need to be a perfect, comprehensive plan. The goal isn't perfection, it's just progress.

For many, estate planning sounds like wealth management is only for wealthy people with large estates. I define estate planning as completing the paperwork for asset management, division, and advanced care stage directives. They're the legal steps made to protect yourself and your assets. You can find empowerment, make your wishes clear and enforceable, and possibly avoid family drama by addressing this paperwork proactively.

You or your loved ones don't need to invest much time and effort into the plan—something is better than nothing. You can even think of it as a spare tire in the back of the car.

One of the best ways to ease into estate planning is to leverage your community. It helps to face the prospect and implications if you are with someone you trust. When my clients are overwhelmed and/or nervous, I also offer to go to their attorney meeting. I have my assistant coordinate schedules, we prefill any paperwork we can, and then we knock it out together. Sometimes, offering to accompany them to their appointment motivates people to make their estate planning appointment.

It can be daunting and overwhelming to think about tackling everything, but the important thing is to start!

CHAPTER 44 REVIEW

- Confronting mortality won't happen in a day because it's a long, complex journey filled with valid and difficult emotions. This process will look different for everyone.
- As complex and remote as it may seem, creating a plan to receive the care you want and need and ease the impossible situation for your loved ones is essential.
- If you are stuck, it helps to reach out to loved ones for support as you start making your plans.

CHAPTER 44 DISCUSSION QUESTIONS

1. Are you resistant to creating an estate plan? If so, why? Can you invite someone to your attorney meeting to discuss your estate plan?

2. How are you feeling toward aging and beyond?

CHAPTER 45

Estate Planning Paperwork—Powers of Attorney, Trusts, and Wills

IN PART 7, you identified who can help care for you and the plans that you would like to have in place. The next area of consideration is the paperwork to enforce your plan and ease the burden for caretakers and loved ones. It's a tangled mess, and one that can get complicated very quickly.

A power of attorney gives someone the power to do things on your behalf as though it's you. The person with your power of attorney may not be the executor of your will. Usually, there is a financial power of attorney and a medical power of attorney, which are documents that specify who can make decisions for you if something happens, such as if you get into a car accident, have a stroke, enter a coma, etc.

Powers of attorney help you while you're alive and then expire upon your passing. They can be broad in general (e.g., Sally can make all of my medical and financial decisions) or specific, like this person is allowed to pick up my medication. The flexibility is endless. This person can take care of my house, but nothing else. This person can touch my finances, but not her brother. It is an important instrument ensuring the people you trust can help you when needed.

Trusts are another legal tool that helps you manage and protect assets. They can assist while you're alive, after your death, or both, depending on how they are structured. In the case of impairment or death, you can establish trusts with very specific instructions. My clients' most commonly used trust is revocable, also known as a living trust.

A living trust allows you to modify it, place assets in it, withdraw assets, live off of trust income, and fully control the trust while you are alive and have mental capacity. The trust will then specify triggering events that dictate who can manage the assets and do things on your behalf. Most often, clients will use incapacity or death as triggering events. An example of how the incapacity event could be set up might be "If I'm disabled, which is to be determined by one family member and a doctor, then my son will have the power to pay my bills, manage my investments, and keep the house cared for until my death."

You would then have the death trigger, which could look something like, "Upon my death, trust assets will be used to pay bills, taxes, and debts owed by me or my estate. Then the assets will be split between my children. Johnny gets the lake house, and Susie gets my jewelry."

Once either event is triggered, the person in charge of the trust is referred to as the trustee. They are only allowed to act under the powers specified in the trust document.

Trusts provide a high degree of control over broader and generous distributions. If a child has disabilities, a substance abuse disorder, or other chronic issues, a trust can be used to limit their access to funds. One client of mine had a daughter with lifelong mental health issues. Under the trust arrangement, the daughter will never get money or assets other than what would be needed for housing, and the payments for housing can only be paid directly to the housing provider. She can't touch the money.

Clients become very concerned about who will serve as their trustee for themselves or their children. Selecting the right people can be particularly daunting in blended families or families that have experienced estrangement. Some family members may be outstanding but struggle with financial management. In such cases, you can appoint a corporate trustee to be the trustee or co-trustee. A corporate trustee usually runs out of a financial institution called a trust company. They have employees who are designated as trustees. If one employee leaves or is fired, another employee is hired. This allows for continuous management of the trust until it is terminated.

Some families see corporate trustees as cold and impersonal. This perception can have both positive and negative aspects. On one hand, it may help avoid an awkward Thanksgiving dinner. If Johnny requests a distribution from the trust and Uncle Jimmy and the trustee denies the request, it can lead to significant tension. Johnny might feel like doing more with the carving knife than just cutting the turkey!

The company makes the decision by appointing a corporate trustee, and the family can avoid interpersonal conflict. Additionally, corporate trustees can be appointed co-trustees with a family member, who must act in agreement with the corporate trustee. This allows for professional help for the trustee and will enable them to "pass the buck" when difficult decisions need to be made or distribution requests are denied.

You can even include specific clauses in the trust specific to pets. If you're worried your dog may not receive the care it needs, you can put money into a trust dedicated to it. For example, my son Sammy will be charged with caring for my dog Snuggles. If Sammy can't take care of Snuggles, my daughter Julie will be in charge. There will be $10,000 set aside so Snuggles does not financially burden either of my children.

Another key feature of living trusts is that all assets within the trust avoid probate. Probate can be lengthy and sometimes expensive, so avoiding probate is a key feature of trusts. Probated assets are public records, making a family's finances available for prying eyes. If you want privacy regarding your assets at your passing, avoid probate by using a trust or other transfer mechanism (like payable on death or transfer on death account designations).

Wills are another legal document that distributes assets and property after one's death. We've all probably seen the reading of a will in movies—a lawyer tells heirs what they will get, and then people in the movie fight! Most clients' estate planning attorneys use a will as a backstop to divert any assets that weren't titled to the trust toward that trust. Sometimes clients forget to do the paperwork needed to change the title to the trust, and the will is there to divert anything overlooked.

Wills can also set up testamentary trusts, which are only active after death. The biggest problem is that they only happen after death, and all assets that pass through the will are subject to state probate laws.

Their biggest weakness is that wills only work when someone is dead! If someone is temporarily sick or permanently disabled, a will does nothing to dictate who should help the infirm individual. That's why we use living trusts with many clients. Wills are more straightforward and typically require less cost and effort upfront, but they miss out on many of the protections, privacy, and control that trusts afford.

CHAPTER 45 REVIEW

- A power of attorney allows someone to make legal, financial, and medical decisions on your behalf.
- Trusts manage assets and can be structured to come into effect during a disabling event and/or death. A living trust allows you to modify, put assets in, pull assets out, live off of trust income, and fully control the trust while you are alive and have mental capacity.

- Wills are another legal document that distributes assets and property after one's death. Many use wills as a backstop for their trusts or to set up only active ones after death. Unlike trusts, wills only come into effect after death.

CHAPTER 45 DISCUSSION QUESTIONS

1. Have you considered who could act as your medical power of attorney or your financial power of attorney in case of an emergency? If so, who are they? Have you communicated this responsibility, and what are your wishes to this person or persons?

2. Whom would you want to make medical decisions for you if you were severely injured? (Name at least two people, in order of succession.)

3. Whom would you want to make end-of-life decisions on your behalf? Same as question 1 or different?

4. Whom would you want to execute your will? (Name at least two people, in order of succession.)

5. If you were to set up a trust, whom would you want to be the trustee for your assets? They may have the responsibility for several years. (Name at least two people, in order of succession.)

CHAPTER 46

Thoughtful Allocation—How to Divide Assets

BEFORE YOU MEET with your lawyers, it helps to identify who should receive specific assets. Take a blank sheet of paper and draw a line down the middle. On the right side, list the people and causes you care about. On the left side, list all your assets. Next, group your assets by type. For example, put all your life insurance policies together, place annuities in another group, and IRAs in another, as these assets are treated differently for estate purposes. Once you get each asset into its category, you can determine what needs to happen for each.

You might have a little brother who plans to become an auto mechanic, which will give him enough money to earn a decent living, but likely not enough for retirement. He won't have a pension, so his only form of long-term income may be Social Security.

Maybe another person on the right side of your paper is going through a difficult separation and has lost most of their money in a bitter divorce. If you want to assist these people with financial support, examine the left side of your paper and determine the best sources for each situation. If you give someone a large sum, you can make them the beneficiary of an account, which will go directly to them.

Suppose you want to give money to two kids, a brother, and a charity. One child is highly responsible with money, so you're not worried. The other has been irresponsible with money. It would be too risky to give them a lot at once. Your brother fell on some hard luck with a tough divorce and has a history of poor decision-making, which has pervaded his personal life and financial situation. The charity has a strong record of transparency, so you don't need to worry.

In this case, we recommend giving people Roth IRAs and life insurance money because those are tax-free. Consider giving traditional IRAs and 401(k) accounts to the charities. If those types of accounts go to people, those people will have to pay taxes, but charities won't. That way, nobody pays taxes on the money, and the contributions can grow. You can ask the attorney and your financial advisor about these nuances as you make your plan.

The most challenging thing about all of this is what messages you send to your family through the allocation of assets you leave behind. For example, if you have three children and two kids want the lake house, but the other kid couldn't care less, how do we make this even? How even should it be? These elements of fairness and family dynamics are the kinds of things that people get stuck on. This is particularly true for questions of managing things during incapacity.

Of course, there is a difference between trying to overcompensate/control the situation and not kicking a hornet's nest. The goal is to handle it in a way that makes it more peaceful. You have to make the call on what you want to do. It's your stuff, not theirs, so you must decide. Being too compliant with what others want will create confusion. If you're stuck, another way to consider this is to focus on what you want to accomplish. What would you like to achieve if your kids were to get a certain amount of money? What do you think that would do for them or not do for them?

Sometimes, we see behaviors from our loved ones that cause us to change the estate planning documents. For example, a client can start distributing everything evenly and fairly. Still, after a beneficiary does something unwise, such as buying a fancy car and falling behind on mortgage payments, they change their wills or trusts to provide greater structure to the money distribution.

However, using wills and trusts as a proxy for healthy communication can be easy. Some people go overboard and change it too much. Suddenly, they're in my office telling me about their son and saying, "He made me mad, so he gets 2% less."

Don't be petty. It is unhealthy to use estate planning as a weapon. If you don't like what your loved one is doing, have an adult conversation with them now, rather than passive-aggressively writing them out of the will so you can "show them when I'm dead." Open up the discussion to repair the relationship while you're alive.

The key is to make sure that none of the accounts conflict. You don't want to accidentally send money to a different person than intended, which happens more often than you might realize. When the legal documents are drafted, it's easy to put the wrong name on accounts. You pay a decent lawyer to make your arrangements, but always double-check everything you sign.

With an idea of how you want to manage and split your assets, you're ready to head to the lawyers to set up your estate plan.

CHAPTER 46 REVIEW

- To start planning the potential division of assets, take a sheet of paper and draw a line down the middle. On the right side, list the people and causes you care about. On the other side, list all your assets and group them by type. You can determine what needs to happen for each.
    - Roth IRAs and life insurance money go to people because those are tax-free. Consider giving traditional IRAs and 401(k) accounts to the charities. If those types of accounts go to people, those people will have to pay taxes, but charities won't. Ask your lawyer for advice to maximize your legacy's impact.
- These decisions can be difficult. If you're stuck, focus on your goal and remember that this is your money. You get to make the decisions.

- While it is your decision, don't be petty and use estate planning as a weapon. Communicate with your loved ones to restore relationships while you're still alive.
- Make sure the accounts don't conflict, and double-check the paperwork before signing.

CHAPTER 46 DISCUSSION QUESTIONS

1. Do the estate asset dividing exercise. Are there still some components you are considering? What are some factors most important to you?

2. Who should receive cash, assets, or business interests if you die? Name the asset and the person who should receive it:

3. Whom do you want to ensure are taken care of in the event of your death? How would you like them to be cared for (college paid off, pay off house, trust that provides income, etc.)?

4. Do you have any assets you want to protect in case your family members get divorced, sued, etc., to ensure they stay in the family or go to people/causes that you care about?

5. Name any charities, causes, or organizations you would like to make donations to through your estate. If you want to donate, name the organization and the dollar amount or percentage.

6. Would you like any safeguards or controls for anyone receiving assets at your passing? For example, if one of your children has ADHD and can't handle money well, a trust that distributes the money slowly over time might be prudent.

7. If you own a business, whom would you like to run it if you had an extended illness or became disabled? If you passed away, would you want the company to stay in the family, or would you like to sell it? Who could buy the business from you?

CHAPTER 47

Emergency Book—A Key During Crisis

IN ADDITION TO the legal paperwork, another documentation tool I highly recommend to clients is an emergency book. An emergency book is a composite of documents that can serve as a lifeline to loved ones in case an emergency happens to you.

These emergency books contain estate documents, copies of power of attorney, advanced medical directives, and account information about investments, bank accounts, and bills. It can include important pet information about the beloved cat with a sensitive stomach, so it doesn't throw up all over the house, or a parrot who will live for 20 more years. I recommend keeping emergency books in a safe, fireproof location in your home, a safe deposit box, or providing your executors or trustees with a copy of the book, if appropriate.

Password books can be helpful or problematic because people update passwords frequently. Some clients use a password keeper on their phone or tied to their email accounts that keeps passwords encrypted. That could allow executors and trustees to access important information quickly if they have access to it. For a complete list of documents and information that I recommend going into the emergency book, please see this chapter's discussion questions..

Once you put together your emergency book, communicate to your loved ones and future caretakers what it is and what it is for. You can talk them through the situations when they need it, and conduct a fire drill, like you did in school when the bell rang and everyone lined up outside. Walk them through what would happen if you were in a health situation or didn't wake up one morning. Help them play it out and talk it out a little bit.

CHAPTER 47 REVIEW

- An emergency book is a composite of documents that can serve as a lifeline to loved ones in case an emergency happens to you.
- These emergency books have estate documents, copies of power of attorney, advanced medical directives, and account information about investments, banks, and bills. They can include other information like important pet care details.
- Password books can be helpful or harmful depending on how frequently they're updated. Access to a phone-based password keeper and/or online email accounts can be invaluable to executors and trustees.
- Once you have put together the emergency book, communicate with your future caretaker what it is, what it's for, and where they can find it in an emergency.

CHAPTER 47 DISCUSSION QUESTIONS

1. Create an emergency book or review its materials if you've created one already. Here is a checklist of documents/information to have in an emergency binder in case of incapacity or death:

    - Wills
    - Trust documents
    - Power of attorney
    - Advanced directives/living will
    - Medical power of attorney/medical proxy
    - HIPAA (Health Insurance Portability and Accountability Act) release forms
    - POLST forms
    - DNR (do not resuscitate) forms
    - Contact information for CPA, financial advisor, attorney, executors, trustees, next of kin, beneficiaries, attending physician, and medical specialists
    - List of accounts at different institutions
    - Password and login list (particularly for bills/utilities, financial institutions, email, and phone)
    - Location of recent tax returns
    - Location of safe deposit boxes
    - List of bills/utilities and payment method (credit cards, auto bill pay)

CHAPTER 48

Legacy of Peace—Estate Planning to Ease Transitions

As MENTIONED IN the previous chapter, setting up estate planning documents can cause a lot of relationship fallout. For example, signing someone up to be a trustee indefinitely on a special needs trust or a spendthrift trust for a drug addict can make Thanksgiving awkward for multiple decades.

With high-drama families that have challenging relationships, having somebody die and throwing money into the mix does not make it better. It's like throwing gasoline *and* dynamite on a fire. There is an ability in some estate documents to have a "poison pill" baked in. If someone contests wills or trusts, they are instantly disinherited, and their portion goes to other heirs or even to charities. "No contest" clauses like this are state-dependent and hard to enforce in wills.

Sometimes I read over documents as a second set of eyes and catch family dynamics that my clients have highlighted. "Didn't you say that these two sisters were fighting? Why are they co-trustees?" I'll ask. "I think we need to talk to the attorney about this." It is essential to continue to evaluate and consider relationships in your estate planning, particularly if you have infrequent estate meetings.

Anne, unfortunately, passed away two years after her fall. Because she used foresight and thought for her estate planning, her sons were able to manage what was a very emotional and overwhelming time. She could live in peace during those years largely because her son could follow her wishes until the end.

Remember that the best plan is any plan that details what you want during this period of life. Estate planning isn't just about organizing assets—it's about creating roadmaps for your loved ones. Proper estate planning can at least somewhat ease the burden we leave behind and provide peace of mind.

CHAPTER 48 REVIEW

- Estate planning can result in relationship turmoil. It can help to have someone familiar with your family dynamics read over your documents.
- Depending on your state and the drama in your family, you may want to consider a "poison pill" to eliminate contestation of wills or trusts. Discuss your options with your attorney if you think it is necessary.
- The best thing that is necessary and wise is the best way to reduce drama and ease strife.

CHAPTER 48 DISCUSSION QUESTIONS

1. What plans do you want to make if you haven't set up your estate plans? Are there any questions you need to ask? Make an appointment with your lawyer to discuss your plans.

2. If you have set up your estate plans, are there any changes you need to make? Are there any questions you need to ask? If it has been a significant amount of time, such as three or more years, make an appointment with your lawyer to review your estate plan.

PART 9

Thriving in Retirement

SUE CAME INTO my office once again recently. She was glowing as she told me about her new life in Corpus Christi. She stopped by to visit some old friends before she went on a trip to Iceland. As she spoke about her new home and grand trip, it was clear that she was having a great time in this phase of life.

I love seeing clients like Sue who have successfully charted a life of happiness in a new era. She has successfully untangled the golden knot of retirement, which many fear to be boring, lonely, or purposeless. Reflecting on Sue, I can't help but think of common patterns among the happiest retirees as they embrace this chapter.

CHAPTER 49

Enjoying the Present—Keys to a Great Retirement

A GREAT RETIREMENT is like a great relationship—each will be different because it is all about finding a great retirement for you. What will make one person very happy and excited may not fit the perfect contours of retirement for someone else. Retirement is another chapter.

Like any part of life, retirement will not always be happy and exciting. It will be difficult at times. Even though there is no one-size-fits-all, perfect retirement, when I see my many clients, some themes lead to a more holistic, happy life.

First, happy retirees are connected to others. They recognize the importance of maintaining social connections throughout retirement, both in breadth and depth. They actively seek opportunities to engage and connect with people with similar interests and values. They prioritize meaningful, face-to-face interactions, whether spending more time with family or joining the neighborhood watch, interest groups, local walking clubs, or political causes.

While they can use online platforms like social media to support these experiences and connections, they go out of their way to see people in physical settings as much as possible. Through these activities, they deepen and expand their social lives, nurture their physical and mental well-being, and provide a sense of purpose.

Second, they stay mentally active. These retirees don't sit idly but find things that stimulate their minds. They find or rediscover enjoyable activities and hobbies and keep their minds sharp. Retirement provides time and space to explore interests in new depth in intellectual and creative pursuits, from astronomy to quilting. This personal growth and new learning grow as retirees develop new skills and stay intellectually engaged.

Retirement also offers the time and capacity to engage in activities that might have been more difficult because of busy work schedules, like attending the grandkids' sporting events. These hobbies, skills, and experiences support fulfillment and social and physical well-being. If you're seeking inspiration, some retirement activities include traveling, gardening, language learning, book clubs, walking groups, and photography. There are few limits to what you can do!

Third, they're physically active as long as they can be, and make an effort to live healthfully. They proactively take care of their health and view their fitness as a journey that requires consistent attention and effort. The first step in this effort is prioritizing exercise. They persistently prioritize exercise three to five times weekly for at least 30 minutes. The type of exercise can be anything from walking the dog to group fitness classes like yoga. Physical fitness keeps the body strong and minimizes stress.

To support their active lifestyles, there are other things that these retirees enjoy, such as whole, healthy foods and staying hydrated throughout the day to support their energy and make them feel well. They moderate their consumption of alcohol, caffeine, and other things because they recognize that balance is essential for a happy life. They prioritize high-quality sleep habits such as steady routines and avoid disruptions that impact their sleep cycle.

Thriving retirees do their best to keep up with their appointments and seek the medical care they require to ensure they are on the best path and in good health. They feel their best by steadily developing and supporting their health in a multipronged and holistic fashion.

Just as these decisions support well-being, some choices tend to bode less well for flourishing in retirement. First, it isn't good when people hang out at home with nothing to do. This can happen during the initial transition to retirement or during other significant life events and crises, like losing a significant other or a health crisis.

While it can be tempting to isolate for an extended period, this reclusive act can often lead to depression. Humans were built to socialize and lead active lives. If you find yourself depressed or otherwise in mental distress, then seek professional help through a therapist or psychologist. As you are able, you can also refer to the tools mentioned earlier in the book to support you on your mental health journey.

CHAPTER 49 REVIEW

- There is no singular path to a happy retirement, but some traits include:
  - Regular, face-to-face socialization.
  - Tending to health, including exercise, sleep, appointments, and eating well.
  - Staying active and pursuing hobbies, skills, and experiences.

CHAPTER 49 DISCUSSION QUESTIONS

1. Reflect on your responses to the previous sections. Are there any areas you still want to develop?

____

____

____

____

____

____

____

2. How can you layer in more socializing with your retirement goals and interests?

CHAPTER 50

Annual Check-Ins—Why Regular Reflection Matters

AMIDST ALL THE activities that can quickly fill retirement life, it can be helpful to pause and conduct a periodic check-in to see what is going well, what is just getting by, and what can be improved. Things can get busy fast in retirement, and there are so many directions it can go, which is why it can help to pause and see how things are developing.

It is helpful to build in space for introspection at the beginning and throughout retirement. Continuing this practice throughout the years of retirement can be valuable for your personal growth and continued well-being. Retirement is a significant life transition that affects all aspects of your life, including your daily routines, significant events, and motivations.

It helps to take time apart from the hubbub and ask yourself: What are you doing? Why are you doing it? How is it affecting you? How is your current lifestyle supporting you, and how could it be better? To touch back on an earlier exercise, what would you see if you were to take a thousand-foot approach and everything was going well?

One effective way to track your introspection is to write in a journal or a digital document. Like the previous exercises throughout this book, you can write your thoughts in a long-form narrative or a bulleted list. Whichever you prefer, take the time to consider these points and write them down, which will help you gain valuable time for reflection. You also have something to look back on and have a point of comparison if you choose to revisit what you've written over time. It's progress that gives life understanding and helps you understand what, if anything, needs to change.

I usually recommend that people reflect once a year. It's an excellent pace for most people. An annual reflection offers a good periodic marker to check how retirement is unfolding and whether you are doing everything you want to do and achieve in retirement. These periodic check-ins prevent you from reinventing the wheel whenever you encounter another life event.

Some people like to do it more or less frequently, particularly if there have been any significant events like a move, a long trip, or a health event. Important life events like these can provide a fresh perspective and change needs. Reflecting on these times can help process and identify whether any changes need to happen.

Ultimately, your preferences and needs should dictate the frequency of these reflections. Things will likely stay static for long periods in retirement, with dynamic intervals when everything changes and constant movement before things fall back into stasis for another spell.

This can be turned into a mini-event within the year, making the exercise purposeful and enjoyable. I have clients who set a time once a year to take a weekend getaway somewhere they love or have a staycation. They use the dedicated time and space to focus and find clarity. It becomes a personal retreat to reflect on the previous year. This allows them to reflect with renewed focus and gives them dedicated time to celebrate their accomplishments and grow excited for the future.

During your periodic check-in, note the things that give your life meaning, particularly the people you spend time with, how you spend your time, and what you enjoy doing. This is also a good time to review your finances and estate plan. Are things on track in the way that you anticipated? If you have a personal financial planner, it can help to set up an appointment with them in the week leading up to your planned reflection so you can have all of the necessary information in hand for you to think through.

A good retirement is about more than just health and wealth—you will have more resilience and robustness if you have those things. It's about having the acuity and ability to shift as life throws you curveballs. Sometimes people get locked into one thing, like boating, woodworking, or whatever they love. It helps to go beyond the interest and see the meaning behind the thing you want to do. Is that thing methodical? Is it because it gives you structure? Is it because it gives you a creative outlet?

Understanding the function that activities play in your life goes beyond the value of self-discovery. It can also assist if you grow beyond a particular hobby. Sewing could be something that you started doing to fulfill a creative itch five years ago. Is it filling the same role now, or is it time to try something new?

As I mentioned previously on hobbies, exploring activities related to something else you have previously enjoyed and thrived in is helpful. Build on your successes. If sewing was your first hobby but isn't fulfilling the role you had for it anymore, then try something related, like quilting or knitting.

This approach allows for expansion and growth without hitting the doldrums. Mental stimulation and development are excellent for longevity and minimizing your risk of dementia. Sudoku doesn't have to be the only way to keep from going crazy, though. The key is to learn something new that sparks your interest and has a manageable frustration threshold. If it's too difficult, it will be less enjoyable and decrease the likelihood that you'll stick with it in the long run.

Building and expanding on existing hobbies also helps in case there is a situation when you cannot continue doing an activity anymore. If you couldn't do your favorite activity anymore, would you be able to respond? If so, how? What could fill the role that activity plays in a way that meets your situation and needs?

Let's pretend that building model airplanes was your hobby because you loved aviation history and the skill required to craft each meticulous model. However, as the years go by, your eyesight bothers you too much, and you struggle to complete models until the fun is gone. Perhaps you are also looking to connect with more people with similar interests. In this scenario, one alternative could be taking a docent position at a local airplane museum and perhaps joining their restoration board. Then, you can continue to build on the knowledge and expertise you have already developed, make new connections, and remain active in a way that meets your needs and capacity.

As you reach for more hobbies and skills as time passes, use the check-in to consider how these interests overlap with other core life areas. Does this lead to more social interaction? Does this support your health?

Think about how your core interest can support your wellness and holistic happiness, leading to new avenues and ways to enjoy your hobby. Sewing is solitary, but quilting clubs allow for more interaction. Dog walking isn't necessarily a communal experience. Walking the dogs at a shelter can enable you to meet more dogs and introduce you to people with similar values and interests. Plus, you also get additional exercise from walking.

CHAPTER 50 REVIEW

- It is helpful to have check-ins at the beginning and throughout retirement. Continuing this practice throughout retirement can be valuable for personal growth and well-being.

- One effective way to track your introspection is to write in a journal or a digital document.
- Within your periodic check-in, note the things that give your life meaning, particularly the people you spend time with, how you spend your time, and what you enjoy doing. This is also a good time to review your finances and estate plan.
- As you consider the things that give your life meaning, ask yourself whether any similar activities might replace existing hobbies if things need to change.

CHAPTER 50 DISCUSSION QUESTIONS

1. Do you do a periodic check-in? If not, when could you start having one?

2. Social connections: Do you have high social connections right now? If not, what can you do to expand and deepen your circle?

3. Mental stimulation: Do you feel like you learn and grow every day? If not, how can you build on or expand existing interests to stay sharp and interested?

4. Physical health: Are you working out at least three times a week? How else are you supporting your health (e.g., sleep, diet, hydration, moderation)? Is there anything you need or want to change?

CHAPTER 51

Adjusting the Sails—Course Correcting After Periodic Check-Ins

PERIODIC CHECK-INS ARE like looking at the dashboard to see whether the check engine light or low tire pressure sensor is on. Even if you notice these things, it's easy to acknowledge them, keep going, and make vague plans that you'll do it later. When you get into the car the next day, you see the light again, and then drive on.

You sometimes need to make a plan to address the issue at hand. Instead of saying you'll put more air in the tire when you have time (and who has time), be specific: "Tomorrow I'm going to put air in my tire, and once a month I will check my tire pressure."

After you complete a periodic check-in, look back on your answers and see what you need to take action on. See what dashboard lights are lit. Note the areas in which you have been procrastinating and where you're unhappy, then make a concrete plan to address them.

You may realize you haven't seen a dentist in three years. Instead of brushing off setting up the appointment for some indefinite future, put it on your calendar and follow through. While getting back on the schedule to see the dentist is simple, the periodic check-in can also be helpful for more vague areas of growth, such as spending more time with family.

When spending more time with family, a key element might be focusing on your grandchildren. To create your plan, you might need to obtain the grandkids' school and sports schedules so you can start arranging a travel itinerary and brainstorming ideas for spending quality time with them. When will you visit? Mark it on the calendars. When will you book the tickets?

Action is the key, especially if you're in a doldrum period, repeating the same thing. Choosing to do something new can interrupt a consistent behavior that you need to change. This is particularly true if you're feeling down, irritable, or not yourself. We usually have feelings for a reason. They serve as our body's check engine lights. You may not know exactly what's causing them. When that happens, run down this list:

- Am I eating right?
- Am I socially connected?

- Am I getting enough sunlight?
- Am I drinking water?
- Am I exercising?
- Am I fulfilled and interested?

If you haven't done anything social in the last four months, you can feel isolated and alone. How can you address that so you're recalibrated? If you're feeling discontent, what's causing it? Then, think about it and schedule things to make changes.

Don't assume the feelings will go away or fix themselves. Almost nothing in life fixes itself. Everything requires a little bit of effort, like gardening. You have to let the plants grow, and you can't just mess with them every day. You still might need to set up a lattice for them, water them, or pull out some weeds. Then, allow them to grow with some attention, and you'll see the results a few months later.

It's a good idea to list activities you need to do, like exercising and socializing. First, it takes time and effort to build meaningful social connections. Finding a common goal or interest helps build meaningful friendships.

Second, having a community aspect to your goals, like consistently working out, can help you achieve better results. Harness peer pressure to achieve your goals. This requires more than just an accountability buddy, which often results in reporting after the fact and isn't very helpful. An accountability partner can take on a confession-like quality. What is more successful is finding someone who supports you through participatory accountability or does the activity with you.

To continue the exercise example, instead of telling someone whether or not you worked out, have someone you meet every morning at the gym. This provides greater motivation and truer accountability than only telling someone.

If reading every day is one of your goals, then once again, having a person who is strictly your accountability partner doesn't help as much as joining a social group like a book club. There is more momentum from a group doing something together instead of telling someone whether you have or haven't done the promised task, which can lead to demoralization and shame.

There will be steady adjustments throughout retirement life, and you will likely be quite busy. The aim is to enjoy this period of life and all the bustle that can come with it. Hold on tight and enjoy the hustle of the golden years!

CHAPTER 51 REVIEW

- After you complete a periodic check-in, look back on your answers and see what you need to take action on.
- Note what you have been procrastinating about and where you're unhappy, then make a concrete plan to address it. Be specific and put it on your calendar.
- If you are feeling vaguely unhappy, don't assume things will get better without some effort. You should consider taking action in one of the following areas:
    - Am I eating right?
    - Am I socially connected?
    - Am I getting enough sunlight?

- Am I drinking water?
- Am I exercising?
- Am I fulfilled and interested?

- One effective way to solidify new habits is to do it with people, such as joining a group.

CHAPTER 51 DISCUSSION QUESTIONS

1. Are there any areas of your life that would benefit from adjusting?

2. Areas to consider when you have an area of your life that needs course correcting:
   a. What will that look like?
   b. When will you do this?
   c. How will you do it?
   d. What are you going to put on the calendar?
   e. What are the steps you need to follow?

3. What is your plan to correct course? Put your plan into action and on your calendar so you can make progress toward the life of your dreams.

CHAPTER 52

A Cup Overflowing—The True Meaning of an Abundant Retirement

ABOUT 80% OF my clientele say they are busier in retirement than they were while working. It's just a different sort of busy, and things quickly add up, particularly if they are taking care of themselves and expanding/deepening their social circles. The hobbies grow in depth and number as do the projects.

Then there are the vacations, visits to grandkids, and doctors' appointments. All at once, they mix until there aren't enough hours for everything they have going on.

While the pace may seem frantic, a healthy busyness can be where fullness is. Ancient writings describe a life of abundance like an overflowing cup or a spring, constantly refilling and replenishing itself.

This fullness is not about being crowded, however, but being dynamic. An abundant life isn't just about quantity but flow and ever-changing quality. Just as a cup or a spring provides life and nourishment, the abundant life gives, receives, and grows.

In contrast, the Dead Sea might seem full but has no life. The water flows in, but doesn't flow out again, so it becomes trapped and desolate. Everything turns to salt, which is the opposite of vitality and growth. Similarly, a life that doesn't give back and has motion, creativity, and connection may still seem full from the outside but feel lifeless on the inside.

A good retirement can sound as simple as getting a house on the beach or buying a boat, but that's not it. The specifics are not as important as why being on the beach or water is essential. Perhaps it could be the exposure to sunlight and exercising frequently, or spending time in nature.

Take opportunities to check in and think about what you want to get out of this season of your life and savor untangling the golden knot!

CHAPTER 52 REVIEW

- Many retirees find themselves busier than during their working years as they balance hobbies, socialize, vacation, and keep up with appointments. With intention and introspection, you can create a fulfilling yet dynamic life, rich with flow and growth.

CHAPTER 52 DISCUSSION QUESTIONS

1. Has your view on retirement changed since the beginning of this workbook? Reflect on the insights you've gained below and what you look forward to doing most in retirement.

Conclusion

Dear Reader,

Retirement isn't an end but a beginning that is rich in possibilities and challenges. It's a time to rediscover yourself and explore your passions. It's a time of growth and self-definition if approached with intention, curiosity, and openness. Still, you will find yourself at a crossroads from time to time. You already built a strong foundation and have been through tough transitions before. This is something you can handle.

The key is to stay engaged with other people, your interests, and your health. Keep checking in periodically throughout retirement, whether you are challenged by switching to enjoying your wealth or navigating changing relationships. Retirement offers incredible choice and flexibility. Before, you were constrained by your career, which dictated where you could live and how you spent your time. You now have the freedom to find joy in what matters to you—family, health, pets, travel, hobbies, and more. It's time to enjoy the freedom you earned through hard work and planning.

This book will be here to reference if you get stuck on this journey. I hope the discussion points will help you now and later if you need to check back in again. The future you want is within reach. Don't let it slip away. Take charge, maximize your financial freedom, and design a retirement that reflects *you*. Don't let anxieties hold you back. You are holding the golden thread. Let's take the next step together.

Happy retirement,

Chris

APPENDIX A

Planning for Retirement 10 Years Out

Year 10:

- Get organized: List all assets and liabilities. In particular, list retirement accounts and other savings and investments. This gives you a starting benchmark and an idea of what your portfolio could do for you during retirement. A general guide is that 4% of your current value would be the amount you could live off of in retirement. This is not a rule—some have argued that the safe withdrawal rate is probably closer to 3% based on interest rates and market valuations.
- Get a general idea of what it will cost to live in retirement by doing a five-minute budget:
    - Add up your take-home pay for your household.

- Subtract any amount you put into savings or investments after tax (do NOT count 401(k) since this comes out before tax).
- Add the amount you got in a tax refund, or subtract the amount you had to pay the IRS when you filed your return.
- Multiply the end result by 1.2 or 1.3, depending on your state, to add it up for taxes. This final number is an estimate of what you would need to live on before taxes.

- Pull the Social Security statement for you and your spouse to get an estimate for your benefit at different ages and check for errors!
- Get a list of pensions you may receive and look at the choices you are given (taking at different ages, survivorship options, etc.)
- Change your asset allocation to be more conservative. A market cycle is typically around five years, so once you are in that window, you need to be more conservative, particularly at the start of retirement. It would be a shame to have saved your whole career, then see your savings be cut in half because of an event like the 2008 financial crisis. Typically, asset allocations between 40% and 60% stocks and the remainder in bonds or fixed-income instruments are appropriate.
- Analyze the following types of insurance and finalize any decisions about them, since their prices increase dramatically in this age range and health concerns start to arise, making premiums more expensive.

  - Long-Term Care Insurance: Premiums have increased dramatically over the last few years, and "rate-ups" (increased premiums) or denials due to health issues have also increased. Many companies have increased their underwriting guidelines, and some have stopped offering new policies altogether!
  - Term and Permanent Life Insurance Contracts: What life insurance do you want to keep through retirement, what policies should end, and when? If you have a pension, will you take survivorship options or use insurance and investments to provide income to your spouse in the event of your death?
  - Survivor or "Second to Die" Insurance Policies: Do you want to leave an inheritance to your heirs or pay estate taxes when you and your spouse have passed away? Second-to-die policies pay out when both spouses are deceased, which lowers mortality risk, making them less expensive.
- If you own a business, you are probably already behind if you haven't developed an exit strategy. This needs to be done ASAP. The larger the company, the longer it takes to sell or exit.

Year 5:

- Get wills and trusts established.
  - Who will make financial/medical decisions for you if you become disabled?
  - Who will inherit your assets? How would you like to protect those assets from predators, creditors, in-laws,

    and outlaws?
    - When should assets be distributed (certain ages etc.)?
- Compile a list of all accounts, belongings, and locations so a survivor could find everything.
- Develop a master list of account logins and passwords.
- Start to analyze any annuity contracts you own and see how they will fit into your retirement spending strategy.
- Do a detailed budget to get a better idea of your current expenses:
    - Use software that connects to your bank and categorizes your spending for you, or look at year-end credit card statements that break things down.
    - If you want to do the "old-fashioned way" with pen and paper, print out three months' worth of checking and credit card statements and take averages. Don't forget to account for once-a-year or twice-a-year payments like property taxes, insurance, and any other fees you have on a schedule other than monthly.
- Take your budget numbers and project how you think they will increase or decrease when you are retired.
- Compare your numbers to your pension: How much isn't covered by your pension and social security? This will come from your investments or part-time work.
- If you are laddering bonds or CDs for spending, make sure the maturities match your spending so you don't have to disrupt your ladder or break CDs and take penalties. Holding bonds to maturity becomes more important in a rising interest rate environment.
- Consider where you want to settle down: Do you want to live in your current home or downsize? Perhaps

"right-size" is a better term. Often, clients will purchase homes that are the same price or comparable in size to their current home, but with better layouts for aging. If you are considering moving, budget for updates to the house to get it ready to sell, and budget for moving expenses. Consider consulting a realtor or a home stager for advice on what would give you the biggest bang for your buck.

- If you move to a new location, how do you plan to develop a new social circle, make new friends, etc.?
- Develop your aging plan: When will you stop driving? Who will make that decision? When will you start taking driving tests to evaluate your ability to drive? Rehab centers offer these. When will you transition from living alone to assisted living? What are the signs of aging so you know when to ask for help? If you plan for these things in advance and discuss them with your spouse and family, the aging process will be more straightforward. There are many uncomfortable discussions to be had during the aging process, and starting early makes things easier, less stressful, and less traumatic.
- Start creating a life plan: Write down with your significant other who you want to be, what you want to have, and what you want to do now and in the future. What are the things that give you joy and meaning? Let's focus on those things and align your money so you can experience them. Multiple studies have pointed to shorter longevity and poor health for those who do not have a plan for what to do with their time after retirement.
- Begin consolidating accounts to make management

easier: roll old 401(k)s into your current employer's plan or an IRA, consolidate your holdings to a few banks or institutions, and consider FDIC insurance for bank accounts. The more accounts you have and the more institutions, the more difficult it is to keep track of everything and use your financial resources effectively.

Year 1:

- Plan your spending for the following year. How much will you spend to live? How many vacations will you take?
- How much will you withdraw from the portfolio? Which account will it come from? What is the tax impact based on where you withdraw from?
- If you plan to transition to part-time work and then full retirement, start networking or looking for job opportunities a year out.
- If you will lose health insurance from work, look at current prices and evaluate your options.
- Decide whether you want to keep the 401(k) plan or roll it over into an IRA.
- If there is a gap for health insurance before Medicare, see whether your employer has any programs for retirees.
- Talk to your spouse about what you want life to look like. If you haven't been spending much time together because of work, it can be a shock to spend a lot of time together again. Open communication is key.

APPENDIX B

Planning for Retirement Five Years Out

Year 5:

- Get organized: List all assets and liabilities. In particular, list retirement accounts and other savings and investments. This gives you a starting benchmark and an idea of what your portfolio could do for you during retirement. A general guideline is that 4% of your current value is the amount you could use to live off of in retirement. This is not a rule—some have argued that the safe withdrawal rate is probably closer to 3% right now, based on interest rates and market valuations.
- Get a general idea of what it will cost to live in retirement by doing a five-minute budget:
  - Add up your take-home pay for your household.

    - Subtract any amount you put into savings or investments after tax (do NOT count 401 (k) since this comes out before tax).
    - Add the amount you got in a tax refund, or subtract the amount you had to pay the IRS when you filed your return.
    - Multiply the end result by 1.2 or 1.3, depending on your state, to add it up for taxes. This final number is an estimate of what you would need to live on before taxes.
- Pull the Social Security statement for you and your spouse to get an estimate for your benefit at different ages and check for errors!
- Get a list of pensions you may receive and look at the choices you are given (taking at different ages, survivorship options, etc.).
- Change your asset allocation to be more conservative. A market cycle is typically around five years, so once you are in that window, you need to be more conservative, particularly at the start of retirement. It would be a shame to have saved your whole career and see your savings cut in half because of an event like the 2008 financial crisis. Typically, asset allocations between 40% and 60% stocks and the remainder in bonds or fixed-income instruments are appropriate.
- Analyze the following types of insurance and finalize any decisions. Their prices increase dramatically in this age range, and health concerns start to arise, making premiums more expensive.
    - Long-Term Care Insurance: Premiums have increased dramatically over the last few years, and "rate-ups"

(increased premiums) or denials due to health issues have also increased. Many companies have increased their underwriting guidelines, and some companies have stopped offering new policies altogether!

- Term and Permanent Life Insurance Contracts: What life insurance do you want to keep through retirement? What policies should end, and when? If you have a pension, will you take survivorship options or use insurance and investments to provide income to your spouse in the event of your death?
- Survivor or "Second-to-Die" Insurance Policies: Do you want to leave an inheritance to heirs or pay estate taxes when you and your spouse pass away? Second-to-die policies pay out when both spouses are deceased, lowering mortality risk and making them less expensive.

- If you own a business, you are probably already behind if you haven't developed an exit strategy. This needs to be done ASAP. The larger the company, the longer it takes to sell or exit.

Year 4:

- Get wills and trusts established.
  - Who will make financial/medical decisions for you if you become disabled?
  - Who will inherit your assets? How would you like to protect those assets from predators, creditors, in-laws, and outlaws?
  - When should assets be distributed (at certain ages, etc.)?

- Compile a list of all accounts and belongings and their locations so a survivor could find everything.
- Develop a master list of account logins and passwords.
- Start to analyze any annuity contracts you own and see how they will fit into your retirement spending strategy.

Year 3:

- Do a detailed budget to get a better idea of your current expenses:
  - Use software that connects to your bank and categorizes your spending for you, or look at year-end credit card statements that break things down.
  - If you want to do it the "old-fashioned way" with pen and paper, print out three months' worth of checking and credit card statements and take averages. Remember to account for once-a-year or twice-a-year payments like property taxes, insurance, and any other costs you have on a schedule other than monthly.
- Take your budget numbers and project how you think they will increase or decrease when you are retired.
- Compare your numbers to your pension: How much isn't covered by your pension and social security? This will come from your investments or part-time work.
- If you are laddering bonds or CDs for spending, make sure the maturities match your spending so you don't have to disrupt your ladder or break CDs and take penalties. Holding bonds to maturity becomes much more important in a rising interest rate environment.

Year 2:

- Think about where you want to settle down: Do you want to live in your current home or downsize? Perhaps "right-size" is a better term. Often, clients will purchase homes that are the same price or comparable in size to their current home, but with better layouts for aging. If you are considering moving, budget for updates to the house to get it ready to sell, and budget for moving expenses. Consider consulting a realtor or a home stager for advice on what would give you the biggest bang for your buck.
- If you move to a new location, how do you plan to develop a new social circle, make new friends, etc.?
- Develop your aging plan: When will you stop driving? Who will make that decision? When will you start taking driving tests to evaluate your ability to drive? Rehab centers offer these. When will you transition from living alone to assisted living? What are the signs of aging so you know when to ask for help? Planning for these things in advance and discussing them with your spouse and family makes the aging process easier. There are many uncomfortable discussions to be had during the aging process, and starting early makes things easier, less stressful, and less traumatic.
- Start doing a life plan: Write down with your significant other who you want to be, what you want to have, and what you want to do now and in the future. What are the things that give you joy and meaning? Let's focus on those things and align your money so you can experience them. Multiple studies have pointed to shorter longevity and

poor health for those who do not have a plan for what to do with their time after retirement.

- Begin consolidating accounts to make management easier: Roll old 401(k)s into your current employer's plan or an IRA, consolidate your holdings to a few banks or institutions, and consider FDIC insurance for bank accounts. The more accounts you have and the more institutions, the more difficult it is to keep track of everything and use your financial resources effectively.

Year 1:

- Plan your spending for the next year. How much will you spend to live? How many vacations will you take?
- How much will you withdraw from the portfolio? Which account will it come from? What is the tax impact based on where you withdraw from?
- If you plan to transition to part-time work and then full retirement, start networking or looking for job opportunities a year out.
- If you will lose health insurance from work, look at current prices and evaluate your options.
- Decide whether you want to keep the 401(k) plan or roll it over into an IRA.
- If there is a gap for health insurance before Medicare, see whether your employer has any programs for retirees.
- Talk to your spouse about what you want life to look like. If you haven't been spending much time together because of work, it can be a shock to spend a lot of time together again. Open communication is key.

www.ingramcontent.com/pod-product-compliance
Ingram Content Group UK Ltd.
Pitfield, Milton Keynes, MK11 3LW, UK
UKHW020122290926
15471UKWH00003B/230

9 798999 13970